dk online

prehistory

London, New York, Melbourne,
Munich, and Delhi

Project Editor Rohan Sinha
Editors Aakriti Singhal, Pankhoori Sinha, Aditi Ray

Senior Editors Claire Nottage, Francesca Baines
Weblink Editors Steven Carton, Niki Foreman, John Bennett
Managing Editor Linda Esposito

Jacket Copywriter Adam Powley
Jacket Editor Mariza O'Keeffe
Jacket Manager Sophia Tampakopoulos

Publishing Manager Andrew Macintyre
Category Publisher Laura Buller

Consultant Professor Michael Benton, University of Bristol

Art Director Shefali Upadhyay
Project Art Editor Romi Chakraborty
Designers Tannishtha Chakraborty, Neha Ahuja, Ivy Roy, Mitun Banerjee

Jacket Designer Neal Cobourne

Senior Art Editor Jacqui Swan
Managing Art Editor Diane Thistlethwaite

DTP Coordinator Sunil Sharma
DTP Designer Harish Aggarwal

Picture Research Marian Pullen
Picture Librarian Claire Bowers
Production Erica Rosen

First published in the United States in 2008
by DK Publishing, 375 Hudson Street, New York, New York 10014

A catalog record for this book is available from the Library of Congress.

ISBN: 978-0-7566-3460-5 (Paperback)
ISBN: 978-0-7566-3461-2 (Hardback)

Color reproduction by Colourscan, Singapore
Printed in China by Toppan Printing Co. (Shenzen) Ltd.

Discover more at
www.dk.com

dk online

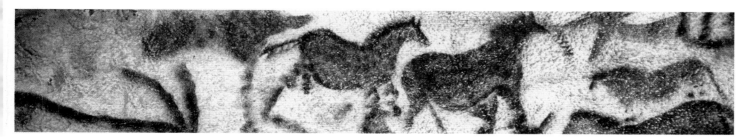

prehistory

Written by **Peter Chrisp**

CONTENTS

How to use the dk online website

dk online prehistory has its own website, created by DK and Google™.
When you look up a subject in the book, the article gives you key facts
and displays a keyword that links you to extra information online. Just
follow these easy steps.

http://www.prehistory.dkonline.com

 **Enter this website address...**

Address : http://www.prehistory.dkonline.com

 **Find the keyword in the book...**

standing stones

 **Enter the keyword...**

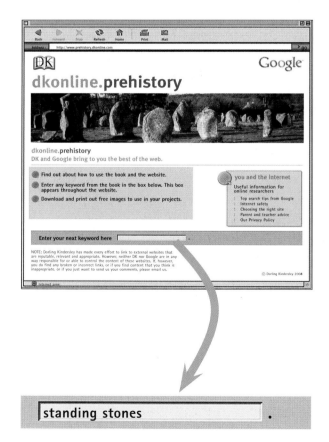

standing stones

You can use only the keywords from the book to search
on our website for the specially selected DK/Google links.

Be safe while you are online:

- Always get permission from an adult before connecting to the Internet.

- Never give out personal information about yourself.

- Never arrange to meet someone you have talked to online.

- If a site asks you to log in with your name or email address, ask permission from an adult first.

- Do not reply to emails from strangers—tell an adult.

Parents: Dorling Kindersley actively and regularly reviews and updates the links. However, content may change. Dorling Kindersley is not responsible for any site but its own. We recommend that children are supervised while online, that they do not use chatrooms, and that filtering software is used to block unsuitable material.

 Click on your chosen link...

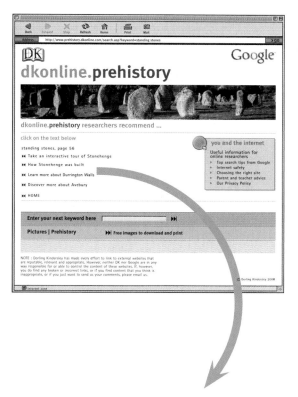

▶▶| **Learn more about Durrington Walls**

Links include animations, videos, sound buttons, virtual tours, interactive quizzes, databases, timelines, and realtime reports.

 Download fantastic pictures...

Pictures | Prehistory ▶▶|

Flint hand-ax

The pictures are free of charge, but can be used for personal, non-commercial use only.

Go back to the book for your next subject...

8

WHAT IS PREHISTORY?

Prehistory is the study of the past before writing or widespread written records. In its widest sense, this period stretches back to the beginning of the universe, about 13.7 billion years ago. But this book is about human prehistory, which began when our apelike ancestors first walked on two legs, perhaps six million years ago. It ended when the last people to live without writing were discovered. Some of humans' greatest achievements were made by prehistoric people. They created the world's first languages, and learned to make tools and clothes and to control fire. They invented art, religion, farming, boats, and the wheel. Prehistoric people also settled the world, from the Arctic to the deserts of Australia.

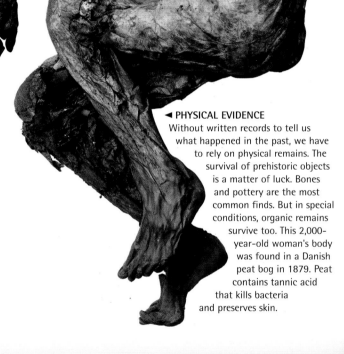

◄ PHYSICAL EVIDENCE
Without written records to tell us what happened in the past, we have to rely on physical remains. The survival of prehistoric objects is a matter of luck. Bones and pottery are the most common finds. But in special conditions, organic remains survive too. This 2,000-year-old woman's body was found in a Danish peat bog in 1879. Peat contains tannic acid that kills bacteria and preserves skin.

PALEOANTHROPOLOGY

The study of human evolution is called paleoanthropology, from the Greek word *palaios* ("ancient"), and "anthropology" (the study of humankind). Paleoanthropologists study the bones of our human and ape ancestors, referred to as hominins. But bones do not reveal all. They cannot tell us when we lost our ape body hair or when different skin colors appeared. Here, paleoanthropologist Richard Leakey (1944–) holds the skull of an early hominin called *Australopithecus*, which lived two million years ago.

▲ HUNTER–GATHERERS

For most of prehistory, people lived by hunting and gathering. There are still hunter-gatherers in some parts of the world today, such as the African bush and desert areas of Australia. Anthropologists study hunter-gatherers, such as these San from southern Africa, to learn how they hunt and make fire, and what their beliefs are. This can help us to understand how our prehistoric ancestors may have lived.

prehistory

▼ THE MYSTERIOUS PAST

Much about prehistory is still unknown, and as a result there are many wild theories. In 1968, writer Erich von Daniken (1935–) claimed that these statues, on Easter Island in the Pacific Ocean, had been built by visitors from outer space. He argued that they could not have been moved by people since no trees grew on the island. In fact, all the trees on Easter Island were cut down to make rollers to move the statues.

▲ AN EVER-CHANGING STORY

New discoveries are still being made that change our view of prehistory. In 2003, an 18,000-year-old hominin was discovered on the Indonesian island of Flores. *Homo floresiensis*, whose skull is shown here, was just 3 ft (1 m) tall and was nicknamed "the Hobbit."

EVIDENCE FROM THE PAST

All the evidence that we have for our prehistoric past comes from material remains—objects and sites—that ancient people have left behind. It is the task of archaeologists to find and interpret this evidence. Many prehistoric sites have been discovered by accident, such as Seahenge in England, an ancient wooden monument revealed by the tide in 1998. Other prehistoric features, including standing stones and burial mounds, stand out in the landscape. The first question archaeologists ask about any prehistoric site is, "How old is it?"

◄ THREE AGES
In 1816, Christian Thomsen (1788–1865), a Danish museum curator, was faced with the problem of organizing his collection of prehistoric artifacts. He reasoned that stone tools, like the sickle on the left, were made before bronze ones (center), and iron tools (right) came last of all. Thomsen suggested dating objects and sites by the three succeeding ages, of Stone, Bronze, and Iron.

BRONZE SICKLE

IRON SICKLE

STONE SICKLE

▲ THE SEAHENGE OAKS
The site of Seahenge, in England, is an upturned oak tree surrounded by a circle of 55 split oak trunks. It was dated to the Bronze Age by dendrochronology—the dating of objects by the study of the annual growth rings of trees. By looking at the pattern of the growth rings of these timbers, archaeologists learned that they were chopped down in the spring or summer of 2049 BCE.

evidence

Different layers have different colors and textures

◄ STRATIGRAPHY
Deep layers of debris accumulate at sites where people have lived for long periods. From the 19th century, archaeologists realized that the deepest layers were usually the oldest. It is possible to place artifacts, such as pottery, in date order depending on their position in the layers. This study of archaeological layers is called stratigraphy.

THE ANCIENT CLIMATE

To understand life in the past, it is useful to reconstruct the whole environment of the period. One method uses snail shells, commonly found in ancient sites. Different snail species thrive in different conditions. By discovering which species were present at a site, we can learn whether the ancient landscape was wet or dry, thick woods or open grassland.

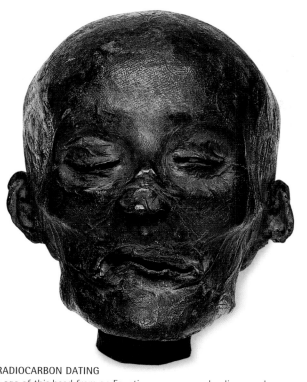

◄ POTASSIUM-ARGON DATING
Potassium-argon dating is a method used at very old sites. It is based on the chemical element potassium-40, found in volcanic rocks, which decays at a very slow rate. It was used to date the oldest stone tools ever found, in the Olduvai Gorge in Africa. By testing the layer of volcanic lava where this stone chopper was found, it was discovered to be two million years old.

▲ RADIOCARBON DATING
The age of this head from an Egyptian mummy can be discovered by radiocarbon dating. All living things absorb the chemical element carbon-14 from cosmic radiation. When they die, the carbon-14 breaks down at a steady, known rate—halving every 5,370 years. By measuring the amount of carbon-14 remaining in this head, we can learn how long ago the person died. This can be used to date organic material up to 40,000 years old.

LOOKING AT ELECTRONS ►
This 4,000-year-old pottery beaker can be dated by thermoluminescence, which uses the ability of clay to absorb and trap minute electrically-charged particles, called electrons. If the clay is heated, electrons are released as light. By heating pottery in a lab, and measuring the light released, we can find out when it was fired or last used as a cooking pot.

WHITE HORSE ▼
This prehistoric figure of a white horse, in Uffington, England, was made by digging trenches, which were then packed with chalk. It was dated by optically stimulated luminescence, a new method that tells us how long ago buried soil was last exposed to sunlight. Soil from these trenches was buried between 1400 BCE and 600 BCE, when the horse was made.

▲ IN GOD'S IMAGE
According to the Bible, God made the world and all living things in six days, and created man and woman on the last day. Humans, made "in God's image," were special and set apart from the rest of nature, which was there for their use. Here God creates the first woman, Eve, from one of the ribs of Adam, the first man.

▲ FATHER OF GEOLOGY
In 1785, a Scotsman, James Hutton (1726–1797), challenged the Bible's account of Earth's age in his paper *The Theory of the Earth*. He argued that Earth was shaped by the same forces in the past that shape it in the present. Rocks were continually being worn away by the weather into sediments, which then form new rocks under heat and pressure. Hutton concluded that the world was much more than 6,000 years old.

DISCOVERING PREHISTORY

Until the early 19th century, people had little idea how old Earth was. The only authority was the Bible, which told the story of human history from the time of the Creation to the time of Christ. This made the world a little over 6,000 years old. Although strange fossils were found in rocks, they were thought to be freaks of nature, or creatures killed in the Great Flood described in the Bible. Then, in the late 18th century, a new science called geology—the study of the history of rocks—changed everything.

◄ A YOUNG EARTH
In the 1640s, James Ussher (1581–1656), the Archbishop of Armagh in Ireland, decided to calculate Earth's age. He did this by counting the generations from Adam to Christ. He concluded that the world had been created in 4004 BCE. A later scholar narrowed this down to 9 am on October 23! From 1700, this date started appearing on the opening page of the Bible, next to the words, "In the beginning God created the Heaven and the Earth." Here, God looks down on his creation.

prehistory

FOSSIL LAYERS

In the 1790s, English engineer William Smith (1769–1839) was building canals across the country. He noticed that distinct layers of rock were characterized by particular fossils that did not appear in other layers. He tracked these layers all across the country to create Britain's first geological map, shown here. The unanswered question was, why did different layers contain different fossils?

CATASTROPHISM ▶
In the early 1800s, French naturalist Baron Georges Cuvier (1769–1832) suggested that a series of worldwide floods had destroyed all life on the planet. He believed God then restocked Earth with a new set of creatures. Cuvier's theory, called Catastrophism, seemed to explain why different fossils were found in different rock layers, each laid down during a flood. This painting by Irish artist Francis Danby (1793–1861) shows the Great Flood from the Bible.

◀ SHAPED BY ICE
In the 1830s, a Swiss scientist named Louis Agassiz (1807–1873) argued that the European landscape had partly been shaped by glaciers—slowly moving rivers of ice. His evidence included U-shaped valleys where glaciers once flowed, and "erratics"— large boulders, such as this one, found in places where they could not have been formed. This rock was dropped here by a passing glacier. The amazing conclusion was that, at some time in the past, Europe had been covered with ice.

▲ CHARLES LYELL
In 1830, the English geologist Charles Lyell (1797–1875) published an influential book called *The Principles of Geology*. Rejecting both the Bible's account of creation and Catastrophism, Lyell argued that geological processes today are the same as those that existed in the past, and that they were occurring at the same rate. He wrote, "The present is the key to the past."

EVOLUTION

The theory that living things evolve with time, giving rise to new species, was first proposed in the 1790s by English scientist Erasmus Darwin (1731–1802). But there was no convincing explanation as to exactly how a species might evolve. Then, in 1859, Erasmus's grandson Charles Darwin (1809–1882) published *The Origin of Species*, in which he explained that evolution was driven by a process he called "natural selection." Darwin's theory led to the conclusion that humans and apes had evolved from a common ancestor.

▲ CHARLES DARWIN
From 1831 to 1836, Darwin traveled as a young naturalist on the ship HMS *Beagle*, as part of a British scientific expedition. He observed that related species of birds on separate South American islands had changed in different ways. Finches, for example, had evolved beaks of different shapes, depending on the type of food available. The shapes of their beaks had evolved to help them survive.

HOW NATURAL SELECTION WORKS

This is part of Darwin's vast beetle collection, which he started while still a schoolboy. It provides an insight into the way natural selection works. A species is a group of animals that are able to breed and produce fertile offspring. But within a species, individuals vary. Some beetles, for example, are born with darker bodies than others. If a species of beetle finds itself in a new environment, a beetle whose body coloring allows it to blend in more successfully with its background is less likely to be caught by a predator than one that stands out. It will survive to pass on its body coloring to its offspring. In this way, over time, many changes in beetles build up, and new species are created. There are now more than 370,000 known beetle species.

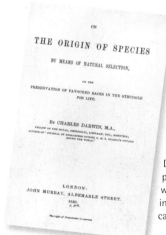

◄ ORIGIN OF SPECIES
Darwin wrote his theory of evolution in 1842, but was reluctant to publish it. He knew that it would shock many Christian readers. It was when another naturalist, Alfred Wallace (1823–1913), came up with the same idea that Darwin decided to go public. *The Origin of Species* was published in 1859. An instant bestseller, it also caused great controversy.

◄ DARWIN'S BULLDOG
English scientist T. H. Huxley (1825–1895) fiercely defended Darwin's theory, and even nicknamed himself "Darwin's bulldog." He also applied the evolution theory to humans. In 1863, he published *Man's Place in Nature*, in which he argued that humans and great apes had evolved from one ancestor. By comparing skeletons (left), he showed that more differences separated lesser apes from gorillas than separated gorillas from humans.

| GIBBON | ORANGUTAN | CHIMPANZEE | GORILLA | MAN |

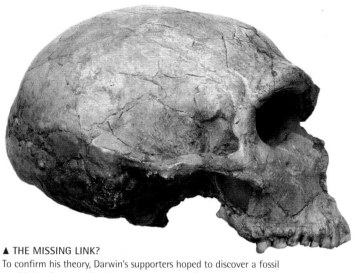

evolution

SEARCHING IN JAVA ►
To find a missing link between apes and humans, you must know where to look. Eugène Dubois (1858–1940), a young Dutchman, thought that the best place to look was the Indonesian island of Java. He believed humans must have evolved in the tropics, and were related to the gibbon (right), which still lives there. In 1887, Dubois set off for Java on his quest.

▲ THE MISSING LINK?
To confirm his theory, Darwin's supporters hoped to discover a fossil combining features of both apes and humans. One possible link was a strange skull that had been found in Germany's Neander Valley in 1856. "Neanderthal Man" looked human, with a large brain case, but had big brow ridges. Scientists concluded that this was not the missing link, but an "inferior race" of modern humans.

JAVA MAN ►
In 1891, Dubois discovered a skull cap (right), in Java, of a human with a brain smaller than the Neanderthal. He named it *Pithecanthropus erectus*, though it was nicknamed "Java Man." It did not have enough ape features to qualify as the "missing link," and scientists dismissed it as that of a modern human. However, Java Man is now accepted as an early human called *Homo erectus* ("upright man").

◄ PILTDOWN MAN
In 1912, a British fossil collector named Charles Dawson (1864–1916) found what seemed to be the missing link at Piltdown in Sussex, England. This was a humanlike skull with an apelike jaw. "Piltdown Man" was accepted as the missing link by British scientists, who are shown in this painting admiring the find. However, it is now known to be a fake—a human skull with an orangutan's jaw, both stained to look old.

THE FIRST STEPS

In 1924, Raymond Dart (1893–1988), an Australian anatomist (scientist who studies the structure of living things), discovered the skull of a genuine "missing link" between humans and apes, at Taung in South Africa. Experts had assumed that the brain was the first human feature to evolve, and expected the missing link to be an ape with a large brain, yet the Taung skull had a brain no bigger than that of a chimp. The reason it qualified as the missing link, however, was that it walked on two legs.

OLDUVAI GORGE ▶
Humans and our bipedal (two-footed) ancestors are called hominins. In the 1950s, a husband-and-wife team of paleoanthropologists, Louis Leakey (1903–1972) and Mary Leakey (1913–1996), discovered more hominin fossils at the Olduvai Gorge, northern Tanzania. This gorge, up to 330 ft (100 m) deep, has preserved more than two million years of prehistory. When hominins lived here, this was a lakeside.

SPECIES OF HOMININS

THE TAUNG CHILD
The skull that Dart discovered in 1924 was that of a three-year-old child, who died 2.5 million years ago. Its most striking feature is that the hole through which the spine enters the skull is centrally placed, like a human's. This means that its head was balanced on the neck, rather than hanging forward like a chimp's, which shows that it walked upright. Dart named his discovery *Australopithecus africanus* ("southern ape from Africa").

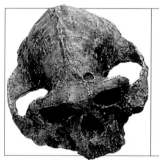

ROBUSTUS
In the 1930s, more australopithecine fossils were found in South Africa, which belonged to a more heavily-built species than the Taung child. As this overhead view shows, the skull has wide cheekbones, big jaws and teeth, and a ridge along the top to which the massive muscles needed for chewing tough plants were attached. It was called *Australopithecus robustus* ("robust southern ape"), and the species lived between 1.8 and 1 million years ago.

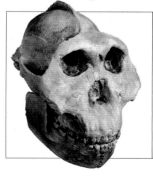

NUTCRACKER MAN
In 1959, Mary Leakey found this skull in the Olduvai Gorge, which she reconstructed from hundreds of fragments. It was another heavily built *Australopithecus*, but different from the South African species. It was named *Australopithecus boisei* in honor of the Leakeys' patron, Charles Boise, and nicknamed "Nutcracker Man" for its massive chewing teeth. It lived between 2.3 and 1.4 million years ago.

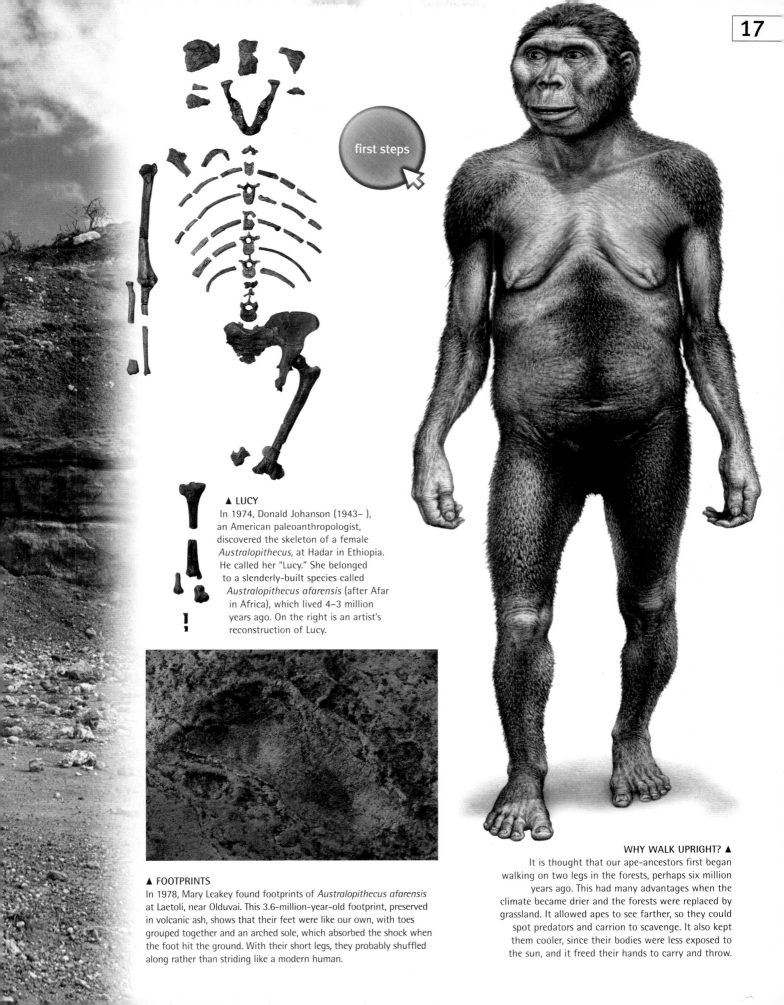

first steps

▲ LUCY

In 1974, Donald Johanson (1943–), an American paleoanthropologist, discovered the skeleton of a female *Australopithecus*, at Hadar in Ethiopia. He called her "Lucy." She belonged to a slenderly-built species called *Australopithecus afarensis* (after Afar in Africa), which lived 4–3 million years ago. On the right is an artist's reconstruction of Lucy.

▲ FOOTPRINTS

In 1978, Mary Leakey found footprints of *Australopithecus afarensis* at Laetoli, near Olduvai. This 3.6-million-year-old footprint, preserved in volcanic ash, shows that their feet were like our own, with toes grouped together and an arched sole, which absorbed the shock when the foot hit the ground. With their short legs, they probably shuffled along rather than striding like a modern human.

WHY WALK UPRIGHT? ▲

It is thought that our ape-ancestors first began walking on two legs in the forests, perhaps six million years ago. This had many advantages when the climate became drier and the forests were replaced by grassland. It allowed apes to see farther, so they could spot predators and carrion to scavenge. It also kept them cooler, since their bodies were less exposed to the sun, and it freed their hands to carry and throw.

THE FIRST TOOLMAKERS

In 1960, Jonathan Leakey (1940–), son of Louis and
Mary Leakey, discovered the skull of an unknown hominin
in the Olduvai Gorge in northern Tanzania. It looked more
human than *Australopithecus*, with a larger brain, flatter
face, and smaller teeth. Its appearance, around
2.5 million years ago, coincides with the first tools made
in prehistory, which the Leakeys also found at Olduvai.
Louis Leakey, was convinced that
this was the first true human.
He named the new species
Homo habilis (handy man).

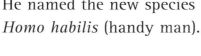

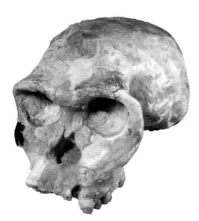

HOMO HABILIS SKULL

▲ HOMO HABILIS
The *Homo habilis* skull above has a brain
capacity of 42 cubic in (687 cubic cm), much
larger than *Australopithecus*, whose brain
was only 33½ cubic in (550 cubic cm) in
volume. However, skeletons show that, like an
ape, *Homo habilis* had long arms and short
legs. The males were around 4 ft (1.2 m)
tall, while the females only reached 3 ft 3
in (1 m). This picture shows *Homo habilis*
with hair like a modern human, but he
may have looked much more like a chimp.

HOMO HABILIS CARRYING
A WOODEN CLUB

THE FIRST TOOLS

CHERT CHOPPER   BASALT CHOPPER

Here are two of the world's oldest tools, made nearly 2.5 million
years ago. They are called Oldowan choppers, after the Olduvai
Gorge. It is likely that these were made by *Homo habilis* rather than
the smaller-brained *Australopithecus*, which also lived here. We
know they are tools rather than naturally-shaped rocks because they
were carried long distances from their sources, and are found mixed
with animal bones. They were made by striking rounded river pebbles
with other stones to produce a cutting edge. Both the chipped
pebble and the removed flakes could be used as tools—the chopper
to smash bones to get to the marrow, and the flakes to cut meat.
Oldowan tools were made from rocks made of crystals, such as basalt
and chert, which are the best materials to give sharp edges. This
shows that the toolmakers had learned to recognize the differences
between types of rock. Wooden tools, such as digging sticks, must
also have been made to get at edible roots and hunt burrowing
animals. Unlike stone tools, these do not survive.

MORE THAN ONE KIND ▶

In 1972, the Leakey's son Richard, who was also a paleoanthropologist, found this 1.9-million-year-old skull by Lake Rudolf in Kenya. It has a flatter, broader face, larger brain, and bigger front teeth than *Homo habilis*. He called it *Homo rudolfensis*. So there were at least two *Homo* species living in East Africa at the same time. Both species are known as habilines because they are so closely related.

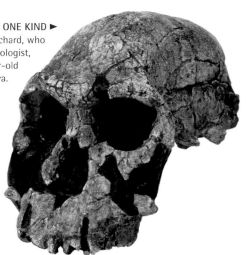

TOOLMAKING APES ▶

Louis Leakey believed that the making of tools by the habilines was a sign that they were human. However, experiments have shown that chimpanzees can also be taught to make and use flaked stone tools. Wild chimpanzees have also been seen using tools, including stones for smashing nuts, twigs to get termites out of their nests, and sticks to dig with. Perhaps the apelike *Australopithecus* also used such tools.

Chimp using a digging stick

▼ HUNTER OR SCAVENGER?

Habilines (*Homo habilis* and *Homo rudolfensis*) had a taste for meat, and their larger brains required animal protein and fat as fuel. They may have been hunters, but it would have been easier for them to get meat by scavenging. They could drive carnivores, such as lions, away from a fresh kill, by throwing rocks and screaming at them. This picture shows habilines that are much more apelike than the interpretation of *Homo habilis* in the picture on the left.

THE FIRST HUMANS

Around 1.9 million years ago, a new kind of hominin evolved in Africa, with a body of the same size and proportions as ours. This new species, called *Homo ergaster* ("working man"), could grow up to 6 ft (1.8 m) tall, and had long legs and short arms. They had larger brains than the earlier, more apelike, habilines, and made much better stone tools. *Homo ergaster* continued to evolve, turning into a bigger-brained form called *Homo erectus* (upright man). This was the first human to leave Africa, moving into Asia. *Homo erectus* also learned how to control fire.

◄ TURKANA BOY
In 1984, Richard Leakey (1944–) found a 1.6-million-year-old skeleton by Lake Turkana in Kenya. It belonged to an 8- to 12-year-old *Homo ergaster* boy. From the neck down, he looks like a modern human with a tall, slim body. His skull combines a human-shaped nose with an apelike flat, low forehead, and a projecting jaw with massive teeth.

humans

OUT OF AFRICA

Sale • Ternifine • Dmanisi • Zhoukoudian
Lantian • Hexian
ASIA
AFRICA
• Awash
Turkana •
• Olduvai
Java
• Swartkrans

● *Homo erectus* finds

Homo ergaster was an early form of *Homo erectus*, whose skull cap Eugène Dubois found in Java in 1891. *Homo erectus* was a human with a brain capacity of up to 76 cubic in (1,250 cubic cm), compared to *ergaster's* 55 cubic in (900 cubic cm). Around 1.8 million years ago, *Homo erectus* moved out of Africa and into Asia. This map shows the main finds of *Homo erectus* fossils. The most important site is Zhoukoudian in China, where the remains of 40 individuals were discovered. The Chinese specimens were nicknamed "Peking Man."

◄ HAND-AX
Homo ergaster ("working man") was named for his toolmaking skills. Around 1.5 million years ago, he invented a tool known as the Acheulian hand-ax. It was made by removing small flakes from a stone to produce a leaf-shaped cutting blade. This was the first stone tool that was cut to a specific shape.

By 700,000 BCE, *Homo erectus* was using fire. The evidence for this comes from the layers of ash and charred animal bones found in caves in China and Israel. Fire provided warmth and light at night, and protected people from predators, such as bears and wolves. It could be used to harden wooden tools and to cook meat. Cooking went on to influence further human evolution as the softer cooked meat no longer required large jaws and teeth to chew with.

NATURAL FIRES
Humans have always been aware of natural bush fires, caused by lightning and lava flows. People probably used natural fire before they were able to light their own. They may have taken smoldering wood from a natural fire to light dry twigs and logs. Once their own fire was lit, they may have kept a piece of charcoal glowing at low heat by wrapping it in dry leaves. They could then have carried this with them when they moved to their next camp. There are still native American people who keep a fire going continuously, with someone to watch over it.

MAKING FIRE
Eventually, people learned to make fire from scratch. Since no firemaking equipment survives from the time of *Homo erectus*, we can only speculate about the method used. The simplest way is to rub wooden sticks together to make a spark. Fire could also be made by striking a flint against a rock containing iron. The spark would light kindling material, such as dry straw or moss, which the firemaker blew on to make the flame grow. Then the fire could be built up, using larger and larger sticks.

FIRST EUROPEANS ▶
The ability to control fire led the descendants of *Homo erectus* to move from Asia to Europe around 500,000 BCE. The first European species was *Homo heidelbergensis*, named after Heidelberg, Germany, where their remains were found in 1908. They were skilled hunters, able to kill elephants and hippos, which lived across Europe at the time, using stone-tipped spears.

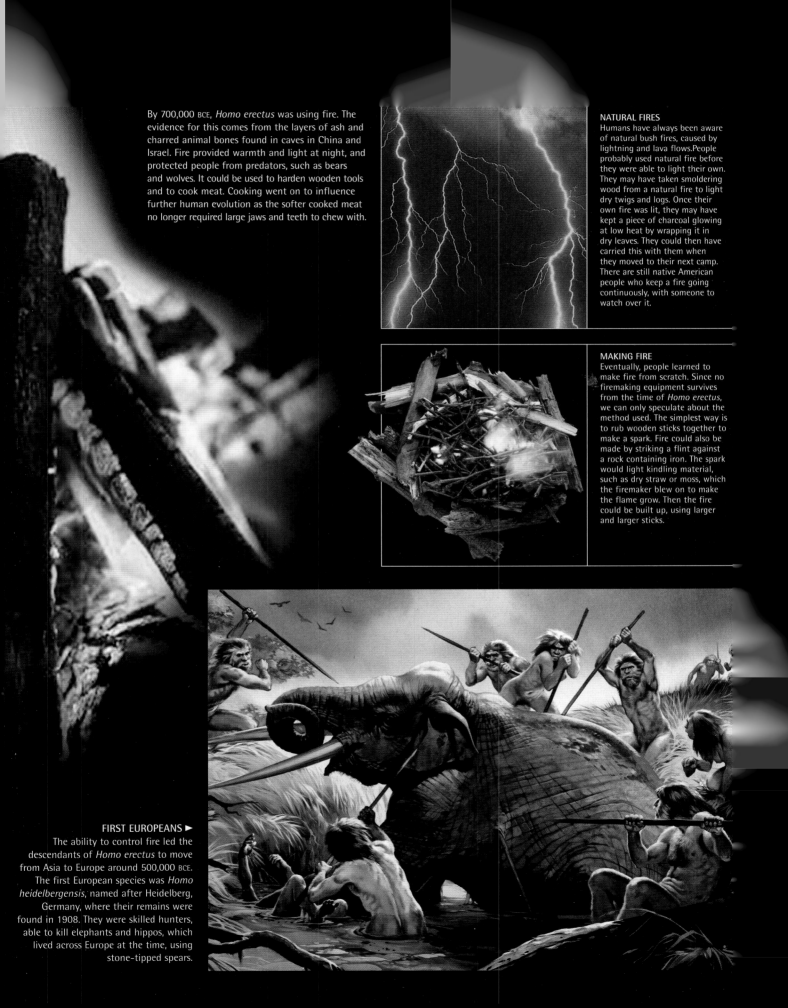

NEANDERTHALS

Around 75,000 years ago, Earth's temperature cooled and ice sheets spread south from the Arctic to cover most northern lands. To the south of the ice, in Europe and western Asia, a region of steppe, or treeless grassland, became home to the Neanderthals—named after the Neander valley in Germany, where their remains were first found. The Neanderthals were stocky, muscular humans, well adapted to cold conditions. They were skilled hunters who made excellent stone tools, dressed in skins, cared for their sick, and buried their dead in caves.

▲ NEANDERTHAL SKULL
You can recognize a Neanderthal skull by its brow ridges, big teeth, weak chin, and huge nasal cavity. Neanderthals had very big noses, which may have helped to warm the air when breathing in. They may simply have chosen mates with big noses because they found them attractive. Their brains were as big as ours, and sometimes slightly bigger.

SKELETON STRENGTH ▶
By comparing the skeletons of a Neanderthal (foreground) and a modern human, we can see that they were much stronger than us. They had broader shoulders, and their forearm bones were wide and curved, an indication of big arm muscles. They needed to be strong, since they lived by hunting dangerous wild animals at close quarters.

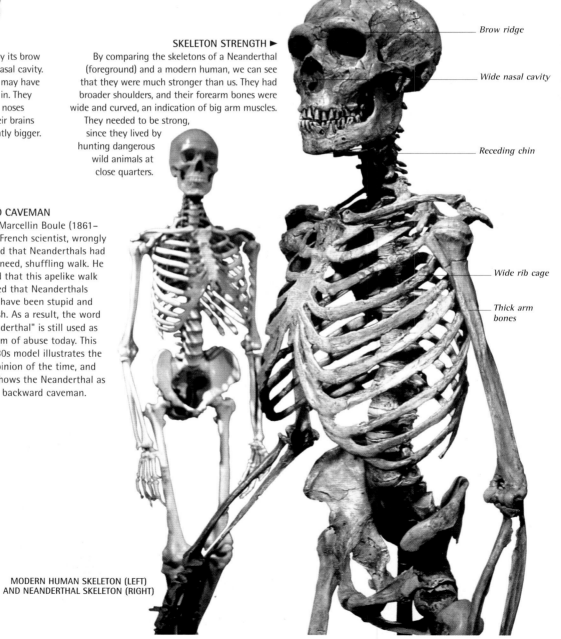

Brow ridge

Wide nasal cavity

Receding chin

Wide rib cage

Thick arm bones

MODERN HUMAN SKELETON (LEFT)
AND NEANDERTHAL SKELETON (RIGHT)

◀ STUPID CAVEMAN
In 1911, Marcellin Boule (1861–1942), a French scientist, wrongly concluded that Neanderthals had a bent-kneed, shuffling walk. He argued that this apelike walk showed that Neanderthals must have been stupid and brutish. As a result, the word "Neanderthal" is still used as a term of abuse today. This 1930s model illustrates the opinion of the time, and shows the Neanderthal as a backward caveman.

TOOL MAKING

CHOOSING A STONE
Neanderthals were skilled at making a wide range of stone tools, including spear points, scrapers, and knives. Using the Neanderthal technique, a toolmaker first chooses a large-sized pebble of chert, flint, or other suitable rock (right), and a smaller pebble to use as a hammer stone.

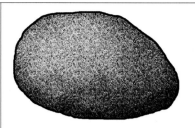

SHAPING THE CORE
The toolmaker strikes the larger pebble around its edges with the hammer stone, knocking off flakes. He strikes two flakes from the top side, creating a ridge down the center, and flattens the far end. This far end is the "striking platform"—a place to hit the stone later to detach flakes.

REMOVING FLAKES
The toolmaker has now struck more flakes from the top. He is preparing the core stone so that a flake of just the right size, shape, and thickness can be removed with a single blow to the striking platform. Many flakes of different shapes and sizes can be made out of a single core stone.

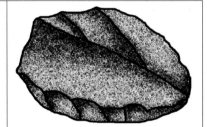

FINISHING
He has now hit the core stone on its striking platform, detaching the flake. From its shape, you can see that it is a point for a spear. More spear points can be made from this same core stone. Neanderthals continued to make tools in much the same way for 250,000 years.

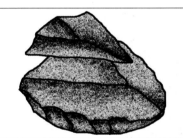

▲ BURIAL OF THE DEAD
The Neanderthals were the first humans to bury their dead in caves, with grave offerings such as flint tools, goat horns, and animal bones. Many skeletons show signs of old injuries that had healed, which reveals that the Neanderthals also cared for their sick. This 60,000-year-old burial of a male, 25–35 years old, was found in 1983 in Israel. He has been nicknamed "Moshe."

Neanderthals

WHAT DID THEY LOOK LIKE? ►
This artist's impression gives a more accurate view of a Neanderthal man than the stupid caveman opposite. Far from walking with a shuffling gait, Neanderthals must have been fast runners. They would have worn warm clothes made from animal skins, tied together with belts. It has been said that a Neanderthal man could pass unnoticed in a crowd today, as long as he had a shower, a shave, and a modern suit of clothes.

TORTOISE CORE ►
The Neanderthal toolmaking technique is known as Levallois flaking, after a site in France where prepared core stones, such as this one, were found. These are known as "tortoise cores" because they resemble turtle shells.

CRO-MAGNON PEOPLE

In 1868, workers laying a railroad track in France discovered the skeletons of four adults and a child in a rock shelter called Cro-Magnon (big hole). The skeletons were 30,000 years old, similar to those of modern humans, and covered with jewelry made of seashells and animal teeth. Since then, more burials have been found, showing that our species, *Homo sapiens* ("wise man"), has lived in Europe since 40,000 BCE. This means that for more than 15,000 years, two types of humans lived in Europe—the Cro-Magnons and the Neanderthals.

▲ NEW CLOTHES

The Cro-Magnons invented needles made of bone (above). Both Cro-Magnons and Neanderthals wore clothing made of animal skins, but, while the Neanderthal's clothes were loosely tied, those of the Cro-Magnon were sewn and decorated with beads. A Cro-Magnon skeleton found in Russia had 2,936 beads sewn onto his clothes.

▲ VARIED DIET

Bones from Cro-Magnon sites show that they had a wider diet than the Neanderthals. They were the first humans to catch fish, using barbed harpoons made of antlers (above). They knew that, in spring, salmon would come up the Dordogne River in France to breed. Many salmon bones have been found in Cro-Magnon sites.

CRO-MAGNON AND NEANDERTHAL

CRO-MAGNON   NEANDERTHAL

These skulls show the difference between the Cro-Magnons and the Neanderthals. The Cro-Magnon had a small, flat, and broad midface, with a smaller nose and a higher forehead. The Neanderthal had pronounced brow ridges and a long, jutting midface, with a large cavity for nose. The jawbones show that the Cro-Magnons had projecting chins, while the Neanderthals' chins receded. The Cro-Magnons' brain case was higher and more rounded than that of the Neanderthals. They had a long, slim body, compared with the short and stocky Neanderthals. We can only guess how the Neanderthals felt about the arrival of the Cro-Magnons. At one Neanderthal site in France, jewelry made of grooved teeth was found, which suggests that they were imitating the Cro-Magnons.

◄ NEW TOOLS

The Cro-Magnons developed new toolmaking techniques, striking off long, thin flakes of flint to make a variety of scrapers, knives, chisels, and borers. They shaped these into specialized tools by retouching. These tools vary regionally, which shows the development of different cultures. The Cro-Magnons were more inventive than Neanderthals, who continued to make the same tools for 25,000 years.

BLADE FOR PIERCING

BLADE FOR CUTTING

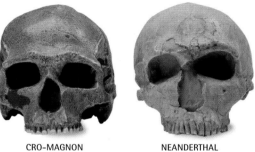

STONES PAINTED WITH
RED OCHER

AMBER NECKLACE

◄ JEWELRY

The Cro-Magnons used their tools to pierce holes in seashells, animal teeth, and other materials to make the world's first jewelry. The seashells, often found far from the sea, also indicate that these people were great travelers. In this way, too, they were very different from the Neanderthals, who preferred to remain in territories they were familiar with.

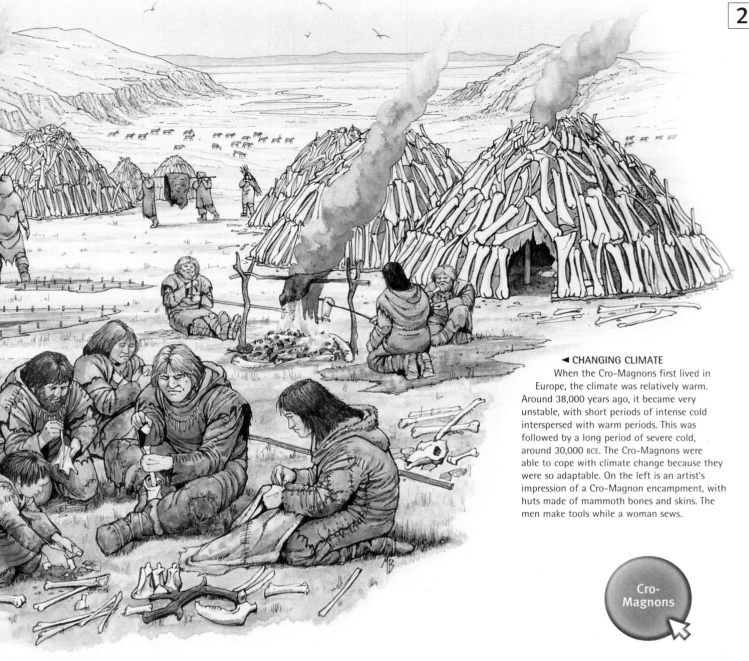

◄ CHANGING CLIMATE
When the Cro-Magnons first lived in Europe, the climate was relatively warm. Around 38,000 years ago, it became very unstable, with short periods of intense cold interspersed with warm periods. This was followed by a long period of severe cold, around 30,000 BCE. The Cro-Magnons were able to cope with climate change because they were so adaptable. On the left is an artist's impression of a Cro-Magnon encampment, with huts made of mammoth bones and skins. The men make tools while a woman sews.

Cro-
Magnons

◄ WHAT HAPPENED TO THE NEANDERTHALS?
The Neanderthals had a harder time coping with the changing climate. They retreated to warmer southern and western Europe and, as they did so, their population plummeted. Although they had survived previous cold periods by retreating to warm areas, they were now competing for resources with the Cro-Magnons. Their last known inhabited site was in these caves, on the island of Gibraltar off southern Spain, where the last Neanderthals lived and died some 24,000 years ago.

HOW DID WE GET HERE?

Today, there is only one human species on the planet. Experts used to think that this was always the case. They believed that the different types of early humans they had discovered, such as *Homo erectus* in Asia and the Neanderthal in Europe, belonged to one species, which had developed regional differences. They thought that modern humans had evolved from the different types of early humans in different places. This was called the "multiregional theory." We now know that this is not true. In fact, there were different species, but *Homo sapiens,* which evolved in Africa, that went on to replace all the other types of human beings.

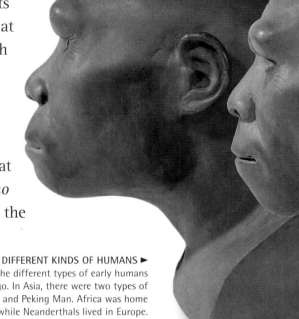

DIFFERENT KINDS OF HUMANS ►
This reconstruction shows the different types of early humans living 130,000 years ago. In Asia, there were two types of *Homo erectus,* Java Man and Peking Man. Africa was home to *Homo rhodesiensis,* while Neanderthals lived in Europe. Multiregionalists argued that modern humans (far right) evolved from the four humans on the left. Now most experts agree that only the African species is our possible ancestor.

JAVA MAN (HOMO ERECTUS)

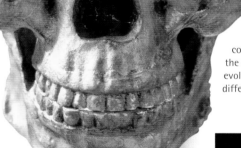

◄ PEKING MAN
This is the skull of Peking Man, a *Homo erectus* found in the 1920s in Zhoukoudian, China. Like modern Chinese people, this skull has a broad, flat face. For Milford Wolpoff (1942–), who continues to be a leading multiregionalist, the skull is evidence that the Chinese people evolved from Peking Man, and that racial differences are very ancient.

DNA EVIDENCE

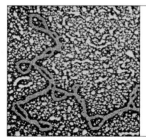

MITOCHONDRIAL DNA
In every living cell are the instructions for its characteristics. These are called genes and they are made up of a chemical called DNA. People's genes come from their parents, but mitochondrial DNA (mtDNA), here in red, passes only from mothers. By comparing mtDNA of different races, scientists can work out when they split apart.

AFRICAN EVE
In 1987, a team of scientists led by Allan Wilson (1934–1991), right, sampled mtDNA from 147 people from different races. The study showed they were closely related, and were all descended from one woman who lived 200,000 years ago. She was nicknamed the "African Eve."

OUT OF AFRICA ►
According to the multiregional theory, Cro-Magnons evolved in Europe from Neanderthals. In the 1980s, however, the British paleoanthropologist Chris Stringer (1947–) studied Neanderthal and Cro-Magnon skeletons and became convinced that they were two different species. He pointed to the tall, slim shape of the Cro-Magnons—evidence that they had evolved in the warm climate of Africa.

HOW DNA IS PASSED ON
The "African Eve" nickname wrongly suggests that she was the only woman alive at the time. There would have been others whose lines of mtDNA have died out. This happens every time a woman has only male children. This diagram shows how mtDNA is passed from mothers on to their offspring.

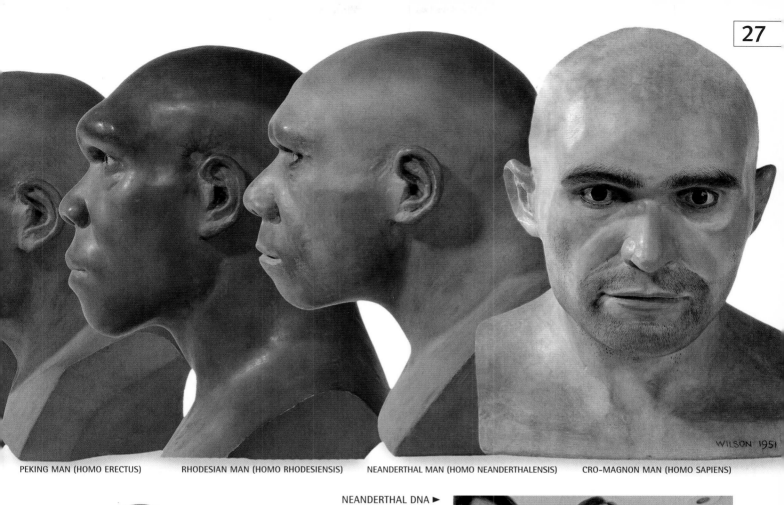

PEKING MAN (HOMO ERECTUS)   RHODESIAN MAN (HOMO RHODESIENSIS)   NEANDERTHAL MAN (HOMO NEANDERTHALENSIS)   CRO-MAGNON MAN (HOMO SAPIENS)

WILSON 1951

NEANDERTHAL DNA ►
This is a team of scientists who have been studying Neanderthal mtDNA extracted from ancient bones. Neanderthal mtDNA, from several individuals, has now been compared with the mtDNA of 10,000 modern Europeans. No living person tested has anything resembling Neanderthal mtDNA. This is strong evidence that the Neanderthals were not our ancestors. The bloodlines of Neanderthals and modern humans separated at least 500,000 years ago.

humans

◄ INTERBREEDING?
Although Neanderthals were a different species from us, it does not mean that interbreeding did not sometimes take place. Donkeys and zebras are also different species, yet, because they are closely related, they can interbreed, though their offspring (left) are infertile. Perhaps Neanderthals and modern humans also interbred, producing only infertile children.

THE FIRST ARTISTS

From 30,000 BCE, the Cro-Magnons in Europe made paintings and sculptures of people and the animals they hunted. This was the world's first art, and it shows a new abstract way of thinking about the world. Abstract thinking is the ability to make a leap in the imagination between the real world and the symbols used to represent it. The mystery about these paintings is that they are found in deep caves, where people would not have lived. The first artists painted their subjects from memory, using only the dim light from stone lamps that burned fat.

▲ LASCAUX HORSE
In 1940, at Lascaux in France, four schoolboys climbed down a hole left by an uprooted tree and discovered a huge complex of caves filled with wall paintings. This beautifully painted horse is just one of the 2,000 figures at Lascaux. The paintings, made around 17,000 BCE, also show stags, bison, and bulls.

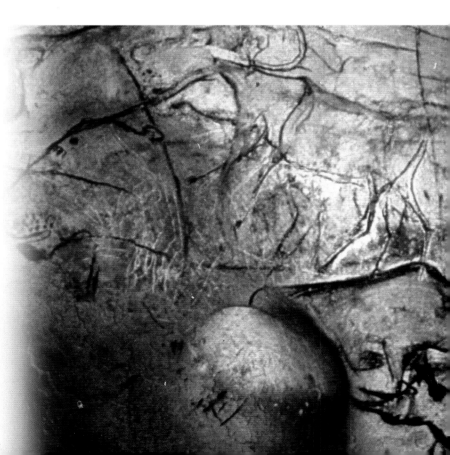

CAVE PAINTINGS ▶
Cave paintings may have been used for ceremonies to bring successful hunting. After being led down a long, dark cave, the men would suddenly have been faced with the images of the animals they would hunt. Usually, only hunted animals appear in cave paintings. However, the Chauvet cave in southern France, discovered in 1994, also showed lions and rhinos (right), which were not hunted. These paintings date from 30,000 BCE.

▲ HANDPRINTS

The cave artists left images of their own hands on the walls. Holding one hand against the cave wall, they sprayed pigment over it, spitting or blowing the colors through a reed pipe. One idea is that the artists were shamans—people who go into a trance to make contact with the spirit world. By pressing their hands against the cave wall, they may have been drawing power from it. Or the artists may simply have been signing their work.

▲ "VENUS" FIGURINES

Female figurines with large, perhaps pregnant, bellies were carved from ivory, antlers, and soft stone. These are found not in caves, but in places where people lived. This figurine is known as the "Venus of Willendorf," discovered in Austria in 1908. It was carved from limestone around 23,000 BCE and is 4¼ in (11 cm) tall.

artists

LION-HUMAN ▶

This mammoth-tusk ivory figure, part lion, part human, was found in 200 fragments in a cave at Hohlenstein-Stadel in Germany in 1931, but only put together in 1969. The carving is 11 in (28 cm) tall and was made around 30,000 BCE. Its purpose remains a mystery. Perhaps it was used in ceremonies by hunters hoping to gain the strength of a lion.

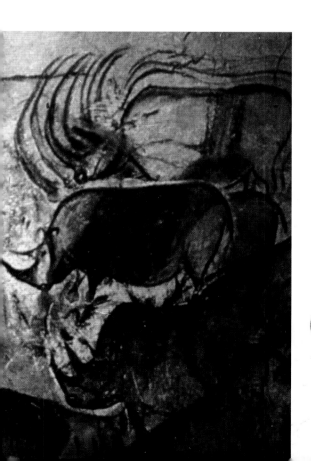

◀ SPEAR-THROWERS

People also turned their hunting equipment into art. A spear-thrower was a stick that lengthened the hunter's throwing arm. The end was often decorated with figures of horses, mammoths, and deer. This piece from a bone spear-thrower shows a mammoth. It may have been carved to help in the hunt, or it may simply have been made as a beautiful object.

MAMMOTH HUNTERS

The woolly mammoth, which lived across Europe, northern Asia, and North America, is the best-known animal of the Ice Age. A relative of modern-day elephants, it had adapted to the cold by developing a coat of long hair and a thick layer of fat beneath its skin. Its small ears prevented the loss of body heat, and its long, sweeping tusks could have been used to clear snow in order to reach plant foods. Mammoths were favored prey of human hunters, providing a large source of meat and plenty of fur for clothing. On the treeless plains, their bones were also used as a substitute for wood. Mammoth bones were burned as fuel, carved to make tools and ornaments, and even used to build houses.

▲ FROZEN BABY
Several mammoths have been found preserved in the frozen soil of Siberia, Russia. The Siberieans had never seen a live mammoth, and used to believe that these creatures lived underground. This baby female, nicknamed "Masha," was discovered in 1988. She has lost most of her woolly coat, although there are still tufts of hair around her feet. Carbon dating shows that Masha died nearly 40,000 years ago, when she was around three months old.

hunters

Tusks could grow up to 16 ft (5 m) long

▲ CAVE PAINTING
Although their remains are rarely found in western Europe, we know that mammoths were common there from cave paintings, such as this one from the Chauvet cave in southern France, discovered in 1994. The many lines sticking out from the shoulder and side of the mammoth in the foreground are thought to represent spears thrown by hunters. This not only confirms that mammoths were hunted, but also reveals the parts of the animal at which hunters aimed their weapons.

HUNTING METHODS

It is still not clear how hunters got close enough to the woolly mammoths to kill them using just their spears. They may have dug pits for traps, although this would have involved a great deal of work, and created the problem of getting the heavy mammoth carcass out of the pit again.

▲ BONE HUT

In 1965, a Ukrainian farmer was digging in his cellar when his spade hit something hard. It turned out to be a mammoth's jaw bone. Further digging revealed 384 more mammoth bones, forming a complete hut. Around 95 animals were killed to make the dwelling, which dates from 13,000 BCE. Curving tusks support the roof, which could have been covered with sod, moss, or mammoth hides.

CARVED IVORY ▶

Mammoth-tusk ivory was carved to make tools, ornaments, whistles, and works of art. This 26,000-year-old carved head is usually described as a female, with her hair in a bun. Yet it could be a man or a woman wearing a hat. The twisted mouth, which droops to one side, suggests that this may be a portrait of a real person. If so, it is probably the world's oldest portrait.

Small ears conserve heat

Museum replica of a mammoth

◀ MAMMOTH EXTINCTION

Mammoths disappeared by the end of the last Ice Age, some 11,000 years ago. The warming climate led to a spread of forests and a loss of the grasslands where these animals lived. As their territory shrank, they became even more vulnerable to human hunting. Yet a population of small mammoths survived on a remote island off northern Siberia, becoming extinct only around 1700 BCE.

SETTLING AUSTRALIA

Before modern humans entered Europe, they had spread from Africa across the warm tropics of Asia. By 50,000 BCE, they had found their way to a new continent—Australia. This was during the Ice Age, when sea levels were low and Australia was much closer to Asia. Even so, the settlement of Australia would still have involved a journey of at least 56 miles (90 km) across open water. This is the earliest evidence of people building seagoing craft, though we do not know what these first boats looked like.

SETTLEMENT ROUTES

SUNDALAND

NEW GUINEA

ICE AGE AUSTRALIA (SAHUL LAND)

PRESENT-DAY AUSTRALIA

When Australia was settled, Asia stretched much farther south and east than it does today (above right). The islands of Java, Sumatra, and Borneo were a part of the Asian mainland, forming an area called Sundaland (above left). Australia and New Guinea were joined together, forming a separate continent called Sahul Land. To get from Sundaland to Sahul Land, people could have taken two routes, shown by the green arrows above. There may have been many crossings, using both routes. The reason we know so little about the first settlers is that the sea has now risen and flooded the areas where they once lived.

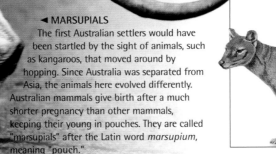

◄ MARSUPIALS

The first Australian settlers would have been startled by the sight of animals, such as kangaroos, that moved around by hopping. Since Australia was separated from Asia, the animals here evolved differently. Australian mammals give birth after a much shorter pregnancy than other mammals, keeping their young in pouches. They are called "marsupials" after the Latin word *marsupium*, meaning "pouch."

EXTINCT ANIMALS OF AUSTRALIA

DIPROTODON
There were no mammoths or rhinos in Australia. Their place was taken by a huge marsupial called a *Diprotodon*, also called a giant wombat. It was as big as a hippopotamus, and grazed the Australian grasslands in herds. *Diprotodon* bones have been found with cut marks on them, indicating that early settlers hunted them. Like many other large mammals, *Diprotodon* was extinct by 22,000 BCE.

GENYORNIS
People also hunted a 6-ft-5-in- (2-m-) tall, flightless bird, called *Genyornis*, nicknamed the "demon duck." It had a huge crushing beak, which suggests it ate meat. It may have been a scavenger, like vultures and carrion crows. By dating *Genyornis* eggshells from many sites, it was found that the bird became extinct within a very short period, some 50,000 years ago. The eggshells came from different climate areas, which suggests that extinction was caused by human hunting rather than climate change.

GIANT KANGAROO
This is the now-extinct giant short-faced kangaroo, which was 10 ft (3 m) tall and weighed 440 lb (200 kg). Like modern kangaroos, it traveled by hopping, which is a very efficient way to move around. Kangaroos can reach speeds of 30 miles (55 km) per hour, which is as fast as a racehorse. The long, heavy tail helps it balance as it leaps. Carrying the baby in its pouch keeps it safe from predators.

THYLACINE
Although marsupials are a separate group of mammals, they evolved in much the same ways as nonmarsupials. The thylacine, for example, looks like a member of the dog family, but is a marsupial. The thylacine became extinct in Australia 2,000 years ago, but survived on the island of Tasmania until the 1930s.

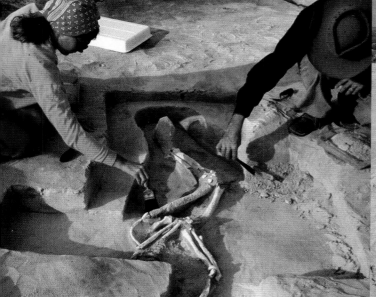

▲ LAKE MUNGO
In 1974, this 40,000-year-old burial was found beside Lake Mungo in southwest Australia. This area, now a dry desert, was once a fertile lakeside, where people hunted kangaroos, caught fish, and collected shellfish. The body, which had been sprinkled with red ocher, is probably male—the parts of the skeleton that would clearly show its gender are missing.

▲ CHANGING CLIMATE
The harsh, cold global climate between 30,000 and 22,000 BCE, which killed off the Neanderthals in Europe, also dried up the lakes and water holes of Australia. The spread of desert was the main cause of the extinction of many large animal species. Ancient ash layers suggest that humans also played a role, by burning the bush as part of their method of hunting. This is Lake Mungo today.

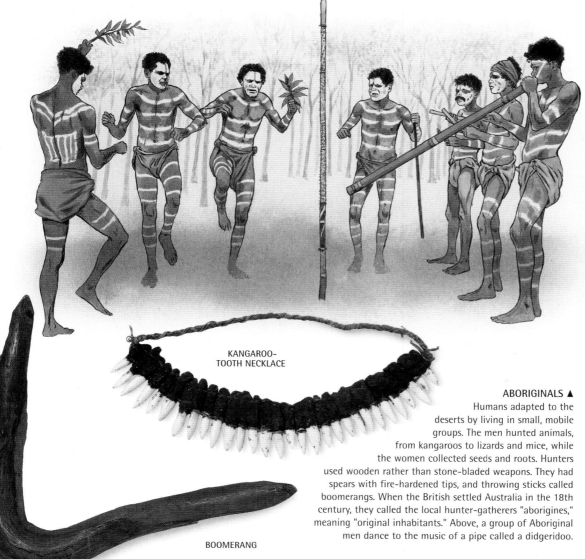

Australia

KANGAROO-
TOOTH NECKLACE

BOOMERANG

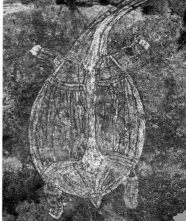

ABORIGINALS ▲
Humans adapted to the deserts by living in small, mobile groups. The men hunted animals, from kangaroos to lizards and mice, while the women collected seeds and roots. Hunters used wooden rather than stone-bladed weapons. They had spears with fire-hardened tips, and throwing sticks called boomerangs. When the British settled Australia in the 18th century, they called the local hunter-gatherers "aborigines," meaning "original inhabitants." Above, a group of Aboriginal men dance to the music of a pipe called a didgeridoo.

▲ ROCK ART
Like the Cro-Magnons of Europe, Australian Aboriginals invented art—painting pictures of animals and spiritual beings on rocks. These are different in style from European cave paintings, which had more realistic images of animals. This painting of a turtle reveals its spine beneath the shell and skin.

SETTLING THE AMERICAS

One of the greatest prehistoric mysteries is the date when people first settled the Americas. This probably happened some time between 30,000 and 14,000 years BCE, during the Ice Age, when sea levels were 200 ft (60 m) lower than they are today, and Asia and North America were joined by a land bridge. DNA tests on modern native Americans, from Alaska to South America, show that they are closely related. Their distinctive tooth shapes also suggest that they are descended from northeast Asians. People had reached the southern tip of the Americas by 13,000 BCE. Following the arrival of humans, several species of large mammals became extinct.

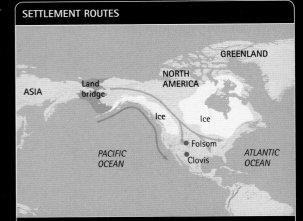

SETTLEMENT ROUTES

The likeliest route taken by the first Americans was overland from East Asia, across the land bridge now called "Beringia." During the Ice Age, this was a grassy steppe grazed by mammoth, bison, and wild horses. Hunters could have crossed over here, following game animals, and then traveled south down an open corridor between the two great ice sheets. Another possible route could have been along the coast, from Asia to North America, following the edge of the ice. Both routes could have been taken, and there may have been several migrations. At the end of the Ice Age, sea levels rose, cutting North America off from Asia.

Americas

◄ CLOVIS
Clovis, New Mexico has given its name to the earliest known North American culture, dating from 11,500 BCE. Clovis people made leaf-shaped blades, which were fluted at the base for mounting onto spears. They were finished by pressure flaking, a method in which small flakes were removed by pressing the tip of an antler against the blade. This allowed greater control of the final shape than striking off flakes. Although Clovis blades are named after this one site, they have been found across the southern US. Clovis people did not stay in one place, but followed herds of animals that migrated seasonally.

◄ HUNTING MAMMOTHS
Clovis blades are often found with bones of mammoths and mastodons – a relation of the mammoth that lived in America. These became extinct at the end of the Ice Age, along with many other large mammals of North America. One possibility, called the "overkill theory," is that Clovis hunters are to blame. But critics of this theory point to the lack of kill sites for other extinct animals. They argue that Clovis people also hunted bison (buffalo), which did not become extinct. They believe the change in climate, as the ice retreated, was responsible.

LA BREA TAR PITS ▲

Ice Age North America was home to many large mammals. We know this from the La Brea tar pits in Los Angeles, California. This was an asphalt (tar) lake, which could have been covered with twigs and foliage, making it look like solid ground. Many animals, including mammoths, mastodons, horses, giant ground sloths, and large saber-toothed cats, became trapped here, and millions of bones have been recovered.

FOLSOM HUNTERS ▶

As the mammoths disappeared, hunters turned to bison. A new hunting culture developed, known as Folsom, after a kill site in New Mexico. Folsom people made lighter stone blades than Clovis people and were specialized bison hunters. These skulls come from a site in Canada called Head-Smashed-in-Buffalo-Jump, where generations of hunters drove herds of bison over a cliff.

KENNEWICK SKULL

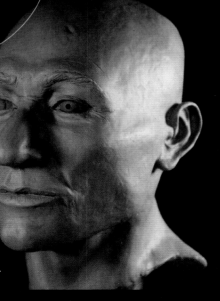

KENNEWICK MAN ▶

Archaeologists have found very few skeletal remains of early native Americans. So the discovery of this skull (above) in 1996 in Kennewick, Washington, caused a sensation. "Kennewick Man" died around 7400 BCE. His skull shape is different from modern native Americans, but resembles Pacific islanders and the Ainu people of Japan, adding to the mystery of how and when North America was settled.

AFTER THE ICE AGE

Around 14,000 years ago, the world's climate warmed. The melting of ice led to a huge increase in open water. New rivers and lakes formed and sea levels rose. With more rainfall, trees began to grow on the dry northern plains. People's lives changed as big game animals disappeared. Now they had to learn to eat new plant foods, to catch more fish, and to hunt smaller animals, such as deer. This period is called the Mesolithic (Middle Stone) Age.

NEW HUNTING AND FISHING METHODS

BOW AND ARROW
The bow and arrow was the ideal weapon for hunting in woodland. It allowed hunters to stalk deer and kill them from a distance. This Spanish cave painting shows Mesolithic hunters using bows.

FISHING
People took to the water in boats made from hollowed-out logs, and fished using lines, traps, and harpoons. This Mesolithic harpoon, made from bone, is barbed so that it sticks in the flesh of a fish.

DOGS
Hunters used dogs to track and bring down deer and boar. The dog was the first wild animal to be domesticated, just before the beginning of Mesolithic period. Here, an African hunter sets off with his dogs.

SICKLE SET WITH FLINT BLADES

BLADE FOR A SICKLE

ARROW HEAD

BARBED ARROW HEAD

SHORT WIDE MICROLITH

LONG POINTED MICROLITH

SHORT POINTED MICROLITH

◄ **NEW TOOLS**
Mesolithic people developed new types of stone tools, including carefully shaped arrow heads. Common finds are tiny stone flakes, called microliths, which were mounted together in wooden or bone handles to make scrapers, or sickles for harvesting plants. Microliths had puzzled archaeologists for a long time. One idea was that they were produced by very small prehistoric people.

PLANT FOODS

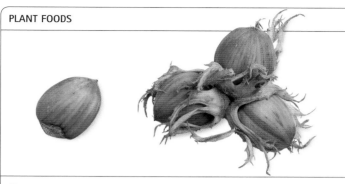

Mesolithic people built up a detailed knowledge of plants, learning by trial and error which ones were poisonous and which were safe to eat. Plant foods, including seeds and nuts, often required special processing. Seeds were ground into flour, mixed with water, and cooked on a hot stone to make flat bread. Hazelnuts (above) were a favorite food, found at many Mesolithic sites. These were roasted to improve their flavor, and to preserve them. Both nuts and seeds were stored in pits for later eating.

▲ MESOLITHIC LANDSCAPE

This Canadian lakeside, surrounded by forest, is an example of a typical Mesolithic landscape. During the preceding Ice Age, this would all have been covered with ice. Such lakesides were favorite places for Mesolithic people to build hunting camps. The water attracts woodland animals, such as deer, to drink. People could gather fruit and nuts from the woods, and fish in the lake.

DEER ANTLERS ▼

At Star Carr in Yorkshire, England, hunters drilled holes in the foreheads of red deer skulls to make antlers they could wear on their heads. One idea is that they wore such antlers as a disguise while stalking animals in the woods. Another suggestion is that they wore them for ritual dances. In modern hunting societies, people sometimes wear masks to impersonate the animals they kill, and contact their spirits.

◄ MESOLITHIC HOUSE

In 2000, archaeologists discovered the post holes of a Mesolithic house at Howick in Northumberland, England. Carbon dating of hazelnut shells showed that it was built around 7800 BCE, and remained in use for at least 100 years. During this period, it was rebuilt twice. We do not know if people used it as a seasonal hunting camp, or lived here throughout the year. The position of the post holes was used to build this reconstruction.

Mesolithic

THE FIRST FARMERS

In the Mesolithic period, people built up knowledge about harvesting wild foods. In the Middle East, they specialized in gathering the seeds of wild grasses. Between 10,000 and 9000 BCE, people learned how to store and sow seeds of plants, which then changed as a result of human selection. Wild wheat has brittle stalks that shatter when ripe, releasing grains to be spread by the wind. People harvested wheat with larger, intact ears, which stayed longer on the plant and eventually created a new wheat with heads that no longer shattered. People also began to control the breeding of animals, such as sheep. They had become farmers. This new period of prehistory is called the Neolithic (New Stone) Age.

SETTLING DOWN ▶
When people became farmers, they were able to settle down in one place, instead of constantly moving in search of wild plants and animals to hunt. On the right is a reconstruction of a house in a Neolithic village from Cyprus, with small, round stone buildings huddled together. By farming, people were able to produce much more food than by hunting and gathering. As a result, population levels rose dramatically.

THE FERTILE CRESCENT

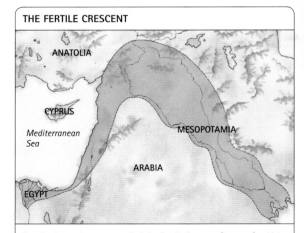

ANATOLIA

CYPRUS

Mediterranean Sea

MESOPOTAMIA

ARABIA

EGYPT

Farming began in an area called the Fertile Crescent (in green), which arched from Egypt in the west around to Mesopotamia in the east. This was an ideal place to farm, because many wild food plants grew here, including emmer and einkorn wheat, barley, rye, chick peas, peas, and lentils. This was also the habitat of wild cows, goats, sheep, and pigs.

EARLY CROPS

EINKORN
Einkorn wheat is one of the early food crops. Its seeds are enclosed in tough husks. The seeds have to be pounded to remove the husks.

EMMER
Emmer wheat has larger grains than einkorn. By 7000 BCE, it had crossed with a wild grass species to produce spelt, a different food plant.

BREAD WHEAT
Around 6500 BCE, spelt further evolved to become bread wheat. Its grains are large, while its husks are soft and easy to remove.

SICKLE
People harvested wheat using sickles made out of wood or antler and set with flint blades. This is an ancient Egyptian sickle.

DOMESTICATING ANIMALS

CATTLE
Animals as well as plants were changed by early farming. Cattle became smaller than their wild ancestors, called aurochs. This was probably because domestic cattle had limited grazing lands and poor winter food. Or people may have preferred smaller animals, which are easier to handle.

GOATS
Wild goats have big scimitar, or sword-shaped, horns. When they were domesticated, their horns became smaller, wider apart, and twisted. These new horns may have been deliberately created by selective breeding. A domestic goat is less likely to injure people than a wild one.

SHEEP
The first sheep were hairy and long-horned and very similar to goats. Following domestication, they lost their long horns and became much more docile. The most dramatic change was that, by 3000 BCE, their soft underhair had grown to become a thick, woolly fleece.

◄ GRINDING GRAIN
Women now spent long hours grinding wheat and barley, using a saddle quern. This was made up of a large, flat lower stone and an upper stone that was pushed back and forth over the grains. Skeletons of women from Tell Abu Hureyra, an early farming village in Syria, had arthritis in the knees and lower spine, and damaged toe and ankle bones. The likely cause was kneeling, with toes bent, over a saddle quern.

farmers

JERICHO ►
In some places, people settled down before they switched from hunting and gathering to farming. Jericho began as a village of Mesolithic hunter-gatherers around 9000 BCE. By 8000 BCE, people were farming. The natives of Jericho built a 10-ft- (3-m-) thick wall around their settlement, with a 30-ft- (9-m-) high stone tower, right. Jericho is the oldest continuously inhabited site in the world.

◄ THE DEAD
The inhabitants of Jericho kept the skulls of the dead in their homes, with features modeled in plaster, and cowrie shells for eyes. This was probably a form of ancestor worship, which is often found in early farming communities. Unlike hunter-gatherers, farmers stay in one place and are strongly aware of the people who lived there before them, farming the same land.

▲ WEAVING
By 7000 BCE, people were making fabric from the flax plant. Its fibers were spun into thread and woven into linen cloth on an upright loom. One set of threads (the warp) was hung from the top beam, kept tight by stone weights, and another thread (the weft) was passed between these. Apart from the stone weights, evidence for early weaving rarely survives. This is a modern reconstruction of an upright loom.

THE INVENTION OF POTTERY

Around 13,000 years ago, people in several parts of the world began using clay to make pots. Pottery was usually invented by farming people, who lived settled lives. It was too heavy and fragile for hunter-gatherers to carry around with them. Pottery was useful because it could be used to carry liquids and boil food over a fire. People also discovered that pottery could be decorative. Beautifully painted vessels became a new way of displaying wealth and status.

▲ POTTERY FIGURINES
People used clay to make figurines long before they made pots. The oldest clay figurines date from 26,000 BCE. This Mesoamerican figurine is of a woman holding two smaller figures. Although they look like babies at first glance, they have the same ear plugs, breasts, and headdresses as the woman.

MAKING A COILED POT

USING CLAY
This is clay soil, a fine-grained material that is easy to shape when it is wet, but hardens when dry. When baked in fire, the clay becomes permanently hard. Prehistoric people may have discovered this property of clay by accident. They probably first used clay to line baskets, in order to make them waterproof. The baskets may have caught fire, making the clay hard.

COIL POTS
This woman is making a coil pot—the oldest and simplest type of pottery. She has rolled clay into long strips, which she uses to build up the top edge of the pot, squeezing the strips into place and smoothing the clay. As she adds the coil with her right hand, she turns the pot with her left. Pots of many shapes and sizes can be made in this way.

FLAT- OR ROUND-BOTTOMED POTS
To prevent the clay from drying out, every few minutes the potter must sprinkle water over the pot. Like many early pots, this one has a round bottom. A round-bottomed pot could be made in a bowl, which made turning easier. Flat-bottomed pots could be placed on mats or large leaves, which were turned. The first potters were probably women, working at home.

BAKED EARTH
The finished pot is placed in a fire and baked. In the process, the gray clay changes to red. Red clay pots, such as this, are called terra-cotta (Italian for "baked earth"). The first pots would have been undecorated like this one. Later, people learned to draw patterns in the surface of the clay, or to paint them with glazes.

▲ JOMON POTTERY

Japan is the only place where pottery was invented by hunter-gathers rather than farmers. The Jomon people made the world's earliest known pottery, around 13,000 BCE. Jomon means "cord patterned," which was a feature of their early pottery. The Jomons made pottery for thousands of years, until 300 BCE. This elaborately decorated pot is from the late period, and was made using a wheel.

CHINESE POTS ▶

This is a Chinese pot, from what archaeologists call the "Yangshao culture." The Yangshao were farming people, who lived by the Yellow River between 5200 and 3000 BCE. Many Yangshao pots were simply decorated, with zigzag patterns. Here, the potter has painted fingers and toes on the zigzag lines, turning them into arms and legs, and added a modeled head.

pottery

POTTER'S WHEEL

The potter's wheel was invented some time before 3000 BCE in Mesopotamia, China, and Egypt. The earliest wheels were simple turntables, which were turned by hand. Later, the wheels had a stick inserted into a notch to turn them more quickly. Wheels made it possible to produce pots on a large scale, and pottery soon became a specialized craft. This figurine of an Egyptian potter dates from around 2750 BCE. He turns the wheel with one hand, while shaping the pot with the other.

◀ ARCHAEOLOGY

Pottery is useful to archaeologists, because it survives while other remains disintegrate. Pots also have distinctive features, such as shape and color, that are useful for dating. In the 1880s, British archaeologist William Flinders Petrie (1858-1942) studied hundreds of Egyptian pots, like this one, and was able to place them in date order. Pottery styles are still used to date Egyptian sites.

THE RUINS OF CATAL HOYUK

RECONSTRUCTION OF THE TOWN

▲ COMPACT BUILDINGS
The rectangular mud-brick buildings were clustered tightly together, and shared walls. There were no doors, so the homes were entered through ladders from the roof. One main room was used for cooking, eating, craftwork, and sleeping on clay side benches with rush matting. The room also had a hearth and a clay oven. Grain was stored in bins in side rooms.

CATAL HOYUK

In 1958, English archaeologist James Mellaart (1925–) dug into a large mound at Catal Hoyuk in Turkey and discovered what was perhaps the first real town in the world. This town must have had a population of several thousand. Catal Hoyuk prospered for more than 1,000 years, from around 7300 to 6200 BCE, and the layers of deposits left by the people who lived here had built up to a depth of 56 ft (17 m). This was caused by the regular rebuilding of the mud-brick houses, and the piling up of garbage. Many houses were decorated with wall paintings, which are the oldest in history.

▲ HUNTING
Although the Catal Hoyuk people were farmers and raised large flocks of sheep, they also hunted wild cattle, red deer, onagers (wild asses), and boars. This wall painting depicts a wild bull being hunted with spears and bows. The bull is much larger than the hunters, which shows how powerful such animals must have seemed.

◀ BURYING THE DEAD
The inhabitants of Catal Hoyuk buried their dead, wrapped in cloth or reed matting, beneath the floors of their houses. One house has been found with 68 skeletons, too many to come from a single family. The mud-brick houses were rebuilt every 70 years. It may perhaps have been a shrine for an extended family or clan.

◄ TRADE

Many materials found in Catal Hoyuk did not come from there, so the town must have been a trade center. Cowrie shells (left) came all the way from the Red Sea, and were made into jewelry. Other goods brought to the town included obsidian, a glassy rock used for making blade tools, and copper and lead, both made into jewelry. Goods manufactured in Catal Hoyuk were probably traded for these raw materials.

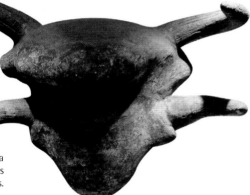

BULL CULT ►

Several Catal Hoyuk houses had rooms with plaster reliefs of bulls, some with real horns and complete skulls from aurochs (wild oxen, now extinct) killed by hunters. Such rooms, which also had freestanding columns and benches mounted with horns, are called Bucrania shrines, from the Latin name for an ox skull.
Mellaart argued that the bull represented a male god who was worshipped at these shrines along with a mother goddess.

◄ MOTHER GODDESS

In one of the grain bins at Catal Hoyuk, Mellaart found a 6½-in- (16-cm-) high clay model of a seated woman (left), whose arms rest on a pair of lions or leopards. He believed her to be a mother goddess, who ensured the fertility of the earth and controlled wild animals, and that she is shown giving birth. Perhaps she had been placed in the bin to protect the grain.

STAMP SEALS

Catal Hoyuk

Mellaart found many small seals, made of pottery and cut with various patterns. Each is 1–2 in (2.5–5 cm) in length. These may have been painted with dyes, and used for printing patterns on fabric. Mellaart found many such seals in the levels of the town without wall paintings. He suggested that the walls there were covered with cloth hangings decorated with stamped patterns. The seals could also have been used to print patterns on bags of goods, as a mark of ownership. People may even have used them to print patterns on their own skin. Yet another theory is that they were not seals at all but counting tokens.

MESOPOTAMIA—THE FIRST CITIES

Mesopotamia means "land between the rivers." These are the Tigris and the Euphrates, which today flow from the mountains of eastern Turkey, across the plains of Iraq to the Persian Gulf. Between 4000 and 3000 BCE, on the southern plain, in a land called Sumer, farming people created the world's first civilization. The villages of Sumer grew into towns and then large cities. In Sumerian cities, the first true temples were built and the first kings ruled from palaces.

▲ CITY GOD
Each city was thought to belong to a god, who was worshipped in a tall mud-brick temple, called a ziggurat. This is the ziggurat in the city of Ur, where Nanna, the moon god, was worshipped. The local people visited the temple for favors and brought offerings. On the plain of Sumer, ziggurats could be seen for miles around, and demonstrated the importance of the god and the power of the city that had built the temple.

THE LAND BETWEEN THE RIVERS

Farming areas (shown in green) spread from northern Mesopotamia, where there was good rainfall, down to the dry plains of Sumer, where people relied on the annual flooding of the Tigris and the Euphrates. Since the flooding took place when crops were already growing, the Sumerians had to channel the water and store it in reservoirs. The Tigris was prone to sudden and disastrous flooding, so people also built high earth banks to protect their homes. This demanded a lot of work and organization, but resulted in surplus food, which meant that many people did not have to farm and could be full-time priests, government officials, or craftworkers. Different classes developed, with the first kings and nobles.

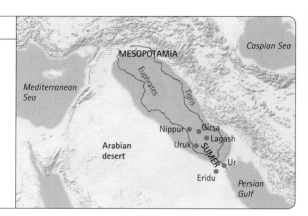

◄ SUMERIAN KINGS
The Sumerians were perhaps the first people to be ruled by kings, who governed on behalf of the city god. This relief shows King Ur-Nanshe of Lagash performing ceremonies during the construction of a temple. The top half depicts him carrying a basket of mud bricks for the building on his head. Beneath, he holds a cup at a banquet marking the temple's opening.

▲ IRRIGATION CANAL
The Sumerians dug canals to carry water from the rivers to store in reservoirs. The water also carried silt, which was left behind after the flood season and had to be regularly dug out of the canals. When the canals were no longer maintained, the land returned to desert.

FARMING

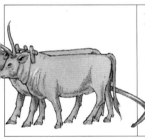

THE PLOW
The Sumerians domesticated oxen, which became their main beast of burden. They also invented the plow, which was used to turn the soil before planting. The farmer walked behind the oxen, holding the wooden plow by its two handles.

DATES
The Sumerians grew dates. These trees are either male or female, and since only the female trees produce fruit, most male trees were cut down for wood. The shortage of male trees meant that farmers had to pollinate the flowers by hand. In this relief, a farmer is rubbing the pollen onto the female flowers.

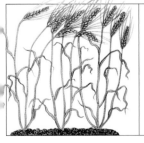

BARLEY
The plains of Mesopotamia are poorly drained. Much of the floodwater evaporated under the hot sun, leaving behind salt that built up in the soil. So the Sumerians grew mainly barley, which is more resistant to salt than wheat. It was used to make bread and beer.

▲ WAR
Sumerian cities were often at war with each other, and their wealth made them a target for invaders. This mosaic from Ur is made of shells, lapis lazuli (a semiprecious stone), and red sandstone. It has the world's oldest image of an army and wheeled transport. It shows foot soldiers with weapons, and chariots pulled by onagers (wild asses).

◄ TRADE
Lacking most raw materials, including metals and precious stones, the Sumerians traded with other lands to get the materials they needed. This is the headdress and jewelry of a woman buried at Ur around 2600 BCE. It is made of imported materials, including gold from Egypt, red carnelian beads from India, and blue lapis lazuli from Afghanistan.

ART AND CRAFTS ▲
Sumerian wealth made it possible for people to work full time as artists, using expensive materials to produce beautiful works for the city rulers. The sculpture above shows a male goat reaching up to eat the golden leaves of a tree, and was found in the same Ur tomb as the woman's headdress on the left.

EGYPT—THE FIRST STATE

While the Sumerians were building their cities beside the Tigris and Euphrates, a second great civilization grew up beside another river that flooded every year. This was the Nile in Egypt. Like the Sumerians, the Egyptians were able to grow so much food that they could support soldiers, priests, and specialist craftsmen. By 3000 BCE, the Egyptians had been united to form a single state, ruled by a king called a pharaoh. The most remarkable thing about the Egyptian civilization is the fact that it continued to exist, with little change, for almost 3,000 years.

▲ THE NILE

Unlike the Mesopotamian rivers, the Nile did not cause catastrophic floods. Its waters rose at the perfect time to plant crops, so the Egyptians did not need to build irrigation canals. The favorable conditions encouraged the belief that the world was ordered by the gods.

◄ BOATS

The river was at the heart of ancient Egyptian life. Goods were transported by reed boats. When people thought of traveling, they thought of boat journeys. They believed that the sun crossed the sky in a boat, and even buried people with model boats (below) to help them travel in the next life.

LAND OF THE NILE

Mediterranean Sea

LOWER EGYPT

Red Sea

Nile

UPPER EGYPT

The Egyptians lived on a long, narrow green strip of land beside the Nile River, with desert on either side. For most Egyptians, this was their whole world—they knew nothing of foreign countries. Between 3500 and 3100 BCE, two kingdoms emerged—Upper (southern) and Lower (northern) Egypt. They were named in this way because the river flows from the south down to the Mediterranean Sea in the north. Around 3000 BCE, a ruler of Upper Egypt conquered Lower Egypt and united the two kingdoms. Although there were towns in Egypt, these were smaller and less densely populated than the Sumerian cities. Protected by the desert, the country was united and usually at peace, so there was no need to build walled cities. Since the whole Nile valley was fertile, each part of Egypt was equally prosperous. The towns that developed were administrative centers, royal capitals, or places where gods were worshipped in temple complexes.

FARMING ►

The year was divided into three seasons—akhet (flood), peret (planting and growth), and shomu (harvest and drought). This wall painting shows farmers at harvest time, with officials called scribes recording the amount of grain gathered. At the top left, people are winnowing grain—tossing it in the air to separate the light husk from the heavier seeds.

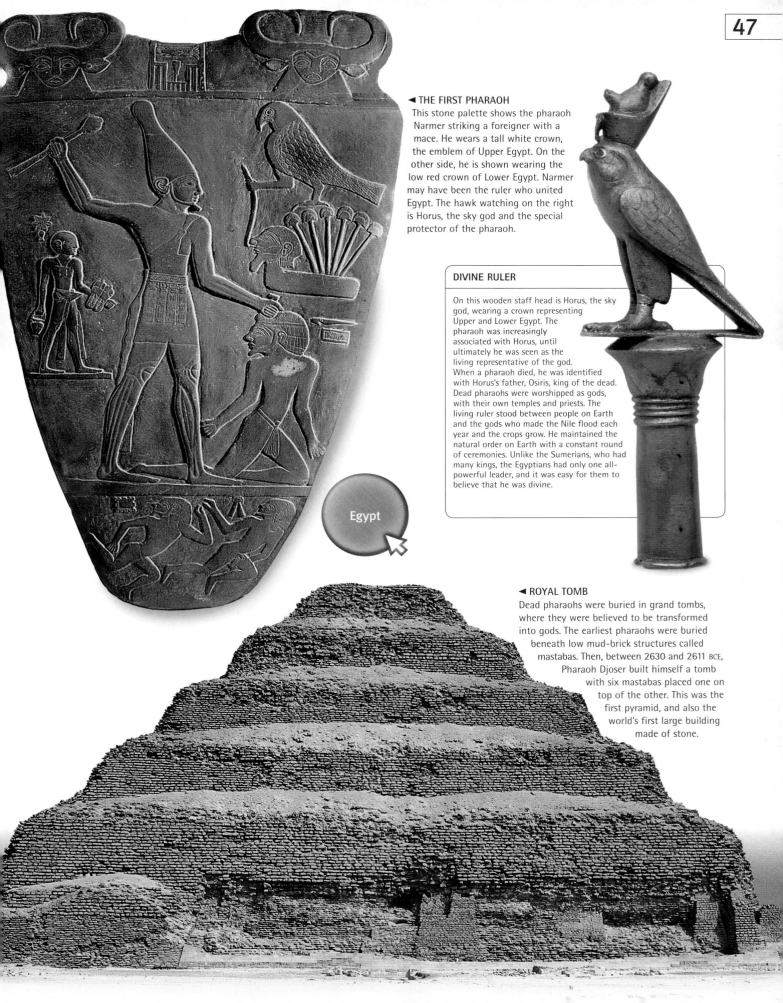

◄ THE FIRST PHARAOH

This stone palette shows the pharaoh Narmer striking a foreigner with a mace. He wears a tall white crown, the emblem of Upper Egypt. On the other side, he is shown wearing the low red crown of Lower Egypt. Narmer may have been the ruler who united Egypt. The hawk watching on the right is Horus, the sky god and the special protector of the pharaoh.

DIVINE RULER

On this wooden staff head is Horus, the sky god, wearing a crown representing Upper and Lower Egypt. The pharaoh was increasingly associated with Horus, until ultimately he was seen as the living representative of the god. When a pharaoh died, he was identified with Horus's father, Osiris, king of the dead. Dead pharaohs were worshipped as gods, with their own temples and priests. The living ruler stood between people on Earth and the gods who made the Nile flood each year and the crops grow. He maintained the natural order on Earth with a constant round of ceremonies. Unlike the Sumerians, who had many kings, the Egyptians had only one all-powerful leader, and it was easy for them to believe that he was divine.

Egypt

◄ ROYAL TOMB

Dead pharaohs were buried in grand tombs, where they were believed to be transformed into gods. The earliest pharaohs were buried beneath low mud-brick structures called mastabas. Then, between 2630 and 2611 BCE, Pharaoh Djoser built himself a tomb with six mastabas placed one on top of the other. This was the first pyramid, and also the world's first large building made of stone.

THE INDUS

Like the rivers of Egypt and Mesopotamia, the Indus of northwest India and Pakistan is a river that floods each year, leaving rich silt for farming. By 2500 BCE, another early civilization had developed here. The Indus people, also called Harappans, built the world's first large planned cities. In other countries, villages grew into towns, which then grew into cities. However, the Indus people planned their cities from scratch. Indus life was highly organized, yet there is no evidence for kings, temples, royal tombs, or warfare.

▼ MOHENJO DARO
These are the ruins of Mohenjo Daro, the best-preserved Indus city. Parallel streets divide the city into blocks, and the main thoroughfares are 33 ft (10 m) wide, exactly twice the size of the side streets. A prominent feature in every Indus city was the Great Bath. This may have had a religious purpose, since bathing has been a feature of later Indian religions.

Indus

THE INDUS REGION

Harappa

Mohenjo Daro

INDIA

Dholavira

Arabian Sea

The Indus civilization (green) covered 485,000 sq miles (780,000 sq km), an area large enough to hold both Egypt and Mesopotamia. Within it a uniform way of life was created, including a shared system of weights and measures, a standard size of bricks, and a common style of pottery. Yet it is not clear how the area was governed—whether it formed a single state, like Egypt, or many separate kingdoms, like Mesopotamia. This map shows the three largest cities, Harappa, Mohenjo Daro, and Dholavira.

The Great Bath

◄ COTTON TRADE

The Harappans were the first people in the world to make clothes from the fibrous seed coats of the cotton plant. Fragments of cloth have been found in Mohenjo Daro. Manufactured cotton textiles were taken to distant lands, such as Mesopotamia and Iran, by merchants. Trade was such an important feature of the Indus civilization that one theory is that it was a state run by merchants.

Seal depicts a unicorn or a bull viewed side-on

▲ WRITING

The Indus people invented a writing system with 300 characters, many of them picture signs, such as the fish at top center here. Writing was used on seals, which were carved in steatite, a soft stone, that was then baked to harden it. Each seal has a picture of an animal, real or imaginary, perhaps representing a particular merchant or family. Indus writing has not yet been deciphered.

Elaborate headdress

◄ DANCING GIRL

This figurine, 4 in (11 cm) tall, was found in 1926 in a house at Mohenjo Daro by the British archaeologist Sir John Marshall (1876–1958). He described her as a dancer who "beats time to the music with her legs and feet." Unlike other Indus female figurines, with elaborate headdresses, she is naked apart from a necklace and bracelets. This suggests that she is not a powerful person and may be a slave girl. But we know so little about the Indus civilization that she could well be a goddess.

Bracelets cover her left arm

◄ CLOTHING

Indus people made terra-cotta models of people, animals, and wheeled carts, which may have been children's toys. These provide us with good evidence for Indus clothing. This woman is wearing a belt, two necklaces, and an elaborate fan-shaped headdress. Such fan-shaped headdresses were often painted black, and one idea is that they represent hair stretched over a frame. Headdresses were decorated with twisted fabrics and ornaments such as flowers.

WHY DID IT COLLAPSE?

While the Egyptian and Mesopotamian civilizations continued, the Indus cities, such as Mohenjo Daro (right) were all abandoned by 1800 BCE. The cause is a great mystery. The collapse may have been caused by flooding, leading to changes in the direction of the rivers. Perhaps the fertility of the fields declined due to overfarming or a build-up of salt in the soil. There may have been a foreign invasion, or a rebellion by the Indus people themselves against their rulers. The cities were buried under silt, and the civilization was forgotten for more than 3,000 years. It was not until the 1920s that a team of British archaeologists, led by Sir John Marshall, rediscovered the lost civilization.

THE FIRST CHINESE FARMERS

Civilization in China developed in fertile river valleys, just as it did in Egypt and Mesopotamia. There were two "cradles" of Chinese civilizations—the Yellow River in the cool north, where millet was cultivated, and the Yangtze River in the warmer and wetter south, where farmers grew rice. By 6000 BCE, the first villages had appeared in these regions. As in the West, the switch from hunting and gathering to farming led to a rapid growth of the population.

◄ FOXTAIL MILLET
This is foxtail millet, which was domesticated by people living along the Yellow River around 7000 BCE. When the grain was domesticated, it lost its ability to scatter the seeds when ripe. Like wheat, millet seeds now wait on the plant until harvested. Grains were ground into flour using stone mortars and pestles.

▲ YELLOW RIVER
This is the Yellow River, which gets its color from yellow silt called loess. During the Ice Age, winds brought the loess here from the Asian steppes. The river carries the mineral-rich loess and deposits it on the North-China plain, where it makes the fields fertile. The water is so thick with silt, one Chinese expression for "never" is "When the Yellow River flows clear."

▲ BANPO VILLAGE
In 1953, some workers building a factory at Banpo, in the central Yellow River region, uncovered an early farming village. This is a modern reconstruction of the village, which was surrounded by a deep defensive ditch and consisted of 45 circular and rectangular houses. The people here grew millet and hemp for fiber, and kept pigs. They also hunted and fished.

◄ MAJIAYAO CULTURE
To the west of Banpo is Majiayao, where, from around 3100 BCE, people started making beautiful pottery vessels. The pots were made by coiling clay, and their surface was smoothed by gently beating it with a flat piece of wood. The top two-thirds of the pot were decorated with black and red patterns, and the bottom third was left plain.

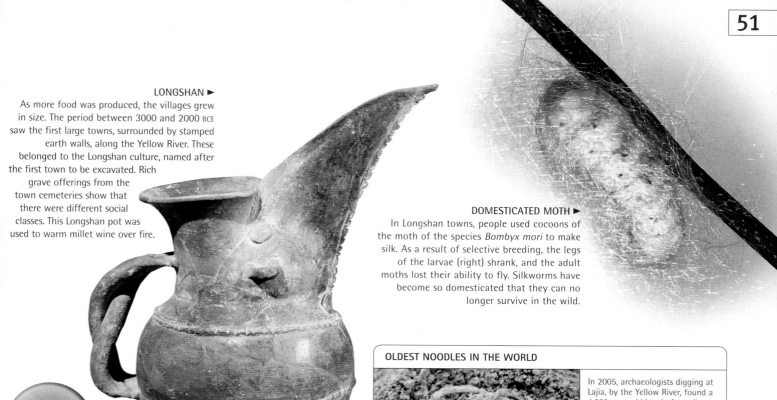

LONGSHAN ►
As more food was produced, the villages grew in size. The period between 3000 and 2000 BCE saw the first large towns, surrounded by stamped earth walls, along the Yellow River. These belonged to the Longshan culture, named after the first town to be excavated. Rich grave offerings from the town cemeteries show that there were different social classes. This Longshan pot was used to warm millet wine over fire.

farmers

DOMESTICATED MOTH ►
In Longshan towns, people used cocoons of the moth of the species *Bombyx mori* to make silk. As a result of selective breeding, the legs of the larvae (right) shrank, and the adult moths lost their ability to fly. Silkworms have become so domesticated that they can no longer survive in the wild.

OLDEST NOODLES IN THE WORLD
In 2005, archaeologists digging at Lajia, by the Yellow River, found a 4,000-year-old bowl of noodles. From the shape of the starch grains, they could tell that these noodles had been made from two varieties of millet. The millet was ground into flour and mixed with water to make dough, which was stretched into 20-in- (50-cm-) long strands, and then boiled. Noodles still form an important part of the Chinese diet. These are the oldest noodles in the world.

▲ YANGTZE RIVER
By around 9000 BCE, people in southern China had domesticated rice from its wild ancestor. Rice farming spread north to the Yangtze River, shown here. Unlike other grains, rice is a marsh plant and thrives in humid, waterlogged conditions. It can grow even in poor soil, as long as there is enough water. Today, rice feeds more than half the world's population.

▲ WET-RICE FARMING
Farmers can grow rice on dry hillside terraces or in flooded fields. The advantage of wet-rice farming is that the water carries nutrients to the plants and stops weed growth. But each rice seedling must be planted individually. As this photograph shows, planting rice is backbreaking work. We do not know when wet-rice farming was first practiced, since flooded fields leave few archaeological traces.

THE FIRST CHINESE CIVILIZATIONS

Around 2000 BCE, the first kingdom appeared in northern China. It was ruled by two dynasties called Xia and Shang (c. 1600–1045 BCE), whose names were first recorded by historian Sima Qian (c. 145–95 BCE) in the 1st century BCE. The dynasties were believed to be mythical until 1899, when "dragon bones," sold as medicine, were found to be turtle shells and ox bones with Shang period writing. In 1928, their source was found to be a royal capital called Anyang. Two features prominent in later Chinese civilizations first appeared here—the worship of ancestors to help the living, and a huge gulf between rulers and ordinary people.

THE SHANG KINGDOM

Yellow River

Huanbei
Zhengzhou Anyang
Sanxingdui
Yangtze

Yellow Sea

East China Sea

■ Shang kingdom

The map shows the area directly ruled, or influenced, by the Shang kings. Huanbei, Anyang, and Zhengzou were three of eight Shang capitals. In 1986, a rival southern kingdom based at Sanxingdui was discovered.

◀ ORACLE BONES
This is one of the so-called "dragon bones" that led to the discovery of the Shang dynasty. They were in fact "oracle bones," used by Shang kings to ask their ancestors questions about the future. The question was written on the bone, and it was burned to produce cracks, which were then interpreted for answers. This is the oldest Chinese writing in existence.

◀ WARFARE
The Shang were often at war with tribes to the north, who raided the kingdom for its wealth. While Shang kings commanded from chariots, most soldiers fought on foot, using bronze halberds. This was a weapon with a blade (left) mounted at an angle on a long pole, held in two hands. Shang soldiers advanced in tight ranks, bristling with a mass of halberds, which they swept down on the heads of their enemies.

◄ HUMAN SACRIFICE
When members of the Shang royal family died, hundreds of slaves and prisoners were sacrificed by beheading, and were buried with them to serve them in the next life. One Shang tomb has 165 dead people in it. This sacrificed charioteer lies stretched out beside his chariot. Human sacrifice was performed not just for the benefit of the dead royal in the tomb, but to demonstrate and confirm the power of the living Shang rulers.

RITUAL CAULDRON ►
Bronze vessels were used in rituals for dead ancestors, who were thought to be able to help the living if they were properly honored. Shang kings offered food and millet wine to their ancestors in vessels like this ritual cauldron, called a "ding." It has three legs because it was placed over a charcoal fire and used to heat food. Such vessels also served as symbols of royal power.

BRONZE ART

BRONZE CASTING
Shang bronzes were made using pottery molds, which were built in several sections, and assembled around a clay core. Molten bronze was poured into the mold, filling the space between the core and the outer sections. This method enabled the Shang to make elaborately shaped and richly decorated bronze works of art, such as this ritual drinking cup, called a "jue."

COPPER AND TIN
Bronze is made from copper and tin, both rare metals. The richest sources in China were around the Shang capital, Anyang, providing a major source of the kingdom's wealth. It was during the Shang period that bronzeworking spread across China. On the right is the bronze tip of a wooden staff, in the form of a human face and a crescent—perhaps the moon or a pair of horns.

EAST AND WEST
Bronzeworking was invented in China and the West at about the same time, between 3500 and 3000 BCE. Chinese bronzeworkers were more skilled at casting the metal. Like all Shang bronzes, this disk, with a man's face in the center, was cast in a mold. In the West, it would have been made by beating a lump of bronze into a sheet and hammering it into shape.

A SOUTHERN RIVAL ►
In 1986, archaeologists excavating at Sanxingdui in southern China discovered two pits filled with elephant tusks, burned bones, jade ornaments, and massive bronzes, which were unlike anything produced by the Shang. This 8-ft-6-in (2.6-m-) tall bronze statue of a man probably once held a curved object, such as an elephant tusk. Sanxingdui may have been part of a kingdom called Shu, which is mentioned in Shang writings.

China

THE MEGALITH BUILDERS

By 4500 BCE, farming had spread from the Middle East to western Europe. The beginning of this new period in prehistory—the Neolithic Age—saw the building of huge stone monuments called megaliths (from the Greek words for "big stone"). Although megaliths came in several different forms, they were all used as communal tombs. It required a massive amount of work, by many people, to build these monuments. Yet the small size of their burial chambers, and the few bones discovered inside them, suggest that they were only used by important people or families.

▲ WEST KENNET
Dolmens were followed by more elaborately built graves, such as this "gallery grave" at West Kennet in England. It has a series of burial chambers off a passage that faces east, toward the rising sun at midsummer. It remained in use for over a thousand years, from 3600 to 2500 BCE.

STONE TABLE ▶
The earliest megaliths are called dolmens, from a Breton word meaning "stone table." Built between 4000 and 3000 BCE, these consist of three or more huge standing stones supporting a larger flat tablestone to create a single burial chamber. Originally, the whole structure was probably covered with a soil or rubble mound. The mounds have since been worn away by the wind and rain.

THE PASSAGE GRAVE

NEWGRANGE PASSAGE GRAVE
One of the most spectacular megalithic monuments is Newgrange in Ireland (c. 3200 BCE), a huge "passage grave" covered by a mound. Within the mound, a long passage leads to an inner burial chamber. The local people's right to farm the land may have been strengthened by the presence of their ancestors in the landscape.

DOORWAY AND LIGHTBOX
This is the entrance to Newgrange. Its outer wall is made of gray granite and white quartz. In front of the entrance is a huge slab decorated with spirals, which were also carved inside the tomb. Above the doorway, there is a second opening, called a lightbox. This was designed to let the sun shine into the tomb.

CORBELED CEILING
The ceiling of Newgrange, shown here, was made by a new method called corbeling. Slabs were placed on top of each other, with each upper layer jutting out over the one beneath. With each layer, the roof opening grew smaller, until it could be covered by a single slab.

megaliths

FRONT OF A SKULL

MACE (CLUB) HEAD

EAGLE TALONS

POTTERY FRAGMENT

▲ BONES AND OFFERINGS
Skeletons found in megalithic tombs are often incomplete, and the bones are jumbled, suggesting that the flesh was removed before burial. Bodies may have been exposed so the crows could pick them clean. This skull was buried around 5,000 years ago, together with animal bones and other offerings, in a burial called the "Tomb of the Eagles" on the island of Orkney, Scotland.

THE SOLSTICE ►
Throughout the year, the sun moves along the horizon, rising in the northeast in midsummer, when days are the longest, and the southeast in midwinter, when days are the shortest. The winter solstice (December 21) marks the southernmost point in its journey, when the sun is weakest. Then it starts moving north and grows in strength, bringing longer days. This "rebirth" of the sun would be celebrated by the Neolithic farmers in northern Europe, with ceremonies to help the sun begin its new journey.

WINTER SOLSTICE AT NEWGRANGE ►
In the 1970s, archaeologists at Newgrange made an amazing discovery. At dawn on the winter solstice, the sun shines through the lightbox into the tomb, lighting the way to the back wall of the burial chamber. People had linked the tomb with the "rebirth" of the sun, which was probably associated with the birth and death cycle, and the spiritual power of ancestors. Perhaps it was during the solstice that bones of those who died each year were placed here.

▲ CAUSEWAYED ENCLOSURES
From 3800 BCE, people across northern Europe built causewayed enclosures—huge circular sites surrounded by one to four concentric ditches, crossed by causeways. These may have been meeting places, where people could trade and hold ceremonies. This enclosure, Windmill Hill in Wiltshire, England, has three ditches. The burial mounds came much later, during the Bronze Age.

STANDING STONES

The most impressive monuments from the Neolithic period in Europe are the standing stones, often arranged in circles or lined up in rows. There are also single standing stones, called menhirs. These were just part of a wider sacred landscape, which included ceremonial walkways, ditched enclosures, and timber circles. These served no practical purpose, and many different theories have been suggested as to why they were built. Often they seem to have been linked with movements of the sun, moon, and stars. Whatever the purpose, the scale and vast amounts of labor involved in the construction of these monuments give us an idea of their importance to the Neolithic people.

◄ DURRINGTON WALLS
The biggest Neolithic monument anywhere in the world is Durrington Walls in Wiltshire, a massive henge, some 1,600 ft (490 m) across. Its bank can be seen from the air. When the road was built here, in 1967, archaeologists discovered a multi-ringed timber circle whose entrance faced sunrise on midwinter day. Animal bones suggest that big crowds gathered here at midwinter to feast.

▲ HENGES
Around 3000 BCE, the idea of creating a special space was taken a step farther with the construction of the henge. This was a circular monument, with a ditch and outer bank. At Thornborough in Yorkshire, England, three identical henges, each 790 ft (240 m) across, were linked by a wide walkway called a cursus. These henges are not in a straight line, and their positions exactly match the three bright stars in the winter constellation of Orion.

standing stones

CARNAC ►
People in Britain built circular monuments, but in northwest France, stones set up in long lines were more common. At Carnac in Brittany, people erected more than 3,000 standing stones in multiple rows. One theory is that each stone was set up to honor an ancestor, whose spirit lived on in the stone. It has also been suggested that they were an observatory, or set up to detect earthquakes.

▲ STONEHENGE

Just 2 miles (3 km) from Durrington Walls, with its timber circle, stands this stone circle, called Stonehenge. Experts believe that the two sites were linked. The timber circle, subject to decay, may have stood for the world of the living, while the permanent and unchanging stones represented dead ancestors.

SUNRISE OR SUNSET? ►

Stonehenge is aligned with both midwinter sunset and midsummer sunrise, illustrated here. The midwinter sunset may have been more important to the Neolithic people. After watching the sunrise at Durrington Walls, they might have come to Stonehenge to see the sun sink behind the stones, as if it was entering the monument.

THE CONSTRUCTION OF STONEHENGE

2950 BCE
Stonehenge was first built as a circular earth bank, 360 ft (110 m) across. This was not a true henge, for the ditch was outside the bank. Just inside the bank, 56 timber posts were set at regular intervals.

2600 BCE
Later, around 80 bluestones (bluish-gray sandstone blocks), each weighing about 4 tons, were brought from the Preselli Mountains in Wales, 240 miles (385 km) away. It is not clear why the builders chose stones from so far away. They set these up in the shape of a double crescent or a horseshoe.

2500 BCE
The bluestones were replaced by gray sarsen stones (hard sandstones), quarried 19 miles (30 km) away. These were set up in a horseshoe of five trilithons (two upright stones with a third on top) surrounded by an outer circle. Bluestones were replaced inside the ring, and more stones placed outside.

HOW WAS IT BUILT? ►

The sarsen stones were shaped at the site by stone hammers, which have been found there. A projection was left on top of each upright, to fit into a lintel (horizontal stone). To lift the lintels, people may have built a wooden platform, which was gradually raised by levering up the ends of each block, and then pushing posts beneath.

Upright is raised using ropes and wooden posts

Each block weighs 25–50 tons

Wooden platform to raise the lintel

Block brought in on wooden rollers

FLINT MINING

Although prehistoric people had always made flint tools, it was not until the Neolithic period that they began to mine flint. By 4300 BCE, Europeans realized that the best-quality flint is found in seams underground. This is because surface flints have been rolled in rivers and glaciers, and damaged by freezing. So people began to dig through the soft chalk, using antler picks, to get the flint. Other hard stones were also mined or cut from quarries. These were made into polished axes, which were traded across Europe.

▲ GRIMES GRAVES
Prehistoric flint mines can be identified by hollow depressions in the ground. These depressions belong to the biggest British flint mine, Grimes Graves in Norfolk, England. Between 1868 and 1870, the English scholar William Greenwell (1820–1918) dug into a hollow and discovered that it was the filled-in shaft of a flint mine. Each of the 433 shafts had been mined for its flint, and then filled with rubble dug from the next shaft.

MINING FLOORSTONE

This picture shows two miners collecting flint in Grimes Graves. At the bottom, you can see a solid layer of black flint, called floorstone. This is the best-quality flint in the mine. The miners ignored two upper layers of flint to get at the glossy black floorstone. Both the flint and the surrounding chalk were formed from the skeletons of marine creatures, which settled on the seabed 100–65 million years ago.

◄ GALLERIES
This photo shows an excavated shaft at Grimes Graves. After digging a wide circular shaft 30 ft (9 m) down to the floorstone layer, the miners carved out seven horizontal galleries (long, narrow passages) around the sides, propping them up with chalk blocks. They worked in these dark galleries by the light of oil lamps made of chalk. Soot stains from the miners' lamps can still be seen on the ceilings of the galleries.

mining

◤ LANGDALE FELL AX FACTORY

This is Langdale, a fell (mountain) in Cumbria, England, where people quarried another type of stone, called volcanic tuff or greenstone. Polished greenstone axes from Langdale were widely traded, and they have been found across England, Wales, and northern Ireland. Perhaps the remoteness of the quarry site was believed to give this greenstone a special power. Many were used just as ornaments or status symbols.

POLISHED STONE AX

◤ DEER ANTLER PICK

This is a red deer antler pick, which miners used to hack through the soft chalk, and to lever out blocks of flint. Hundreds of such picks have been found inside Grimes Graves. They were made out of antlers that were shed naturally by the male red deer. Antler picks have been used as tools for 500,000 years.

POLISHED STONE AX ON A
MODERN WOODEN HANDLE

MAKING A STONE AX

YELLOW QUARTZ AX   BLACK FLINT AX   GLOSSY FLINT AX

As these three examples show, axes were made of different stones. Neolithic people paid special attention to the color and appearance of a stone, as well as its technical qualities. While the rich had polished stone axes as status symbols, most people used rough-flaked axes for practical purposes, such as chopping trees and cutting meat. To make an ax, the rock was struck with a hard hammer stone to knock off the first few flakes. Later, softer wood or antler hammers were used for greater precision. The final shaping was done by pressure flaking, in which a piece of antler was placed against the edge of the stone, and pressure was applied to make small, thin flakes split away.

POLISHED AXES ▶

Around 4000 BCE, people began to grind and polish their axes to give them smooth surfaces. They did this using fine-grained polishing stones or sand and water pastes. It took a long time to polish an ax, and the aim was to make a beautiful object rather than an efficient tool. Some were made from beautifully veined flints, which would have shattered if used as an ax.

THE COPPER AGE

Metalworking started around 7000 BCE, when people in early farming sites, such as Catal Hoyuk in Turkey, began working with naturally occurring gold and copper nuggets. They hammered, cut, and polished the nuggets to make jewelry. Around 5000 BCE, people learned the art of extracting copper by heating its ore (the mineral rock), and pouring it into molds to make tools, or shaping it into pins and bracelets. Unlike stone, metal could be molded and hammered into new shapes. However, copper is a soft metal and tools need continual resharpening. Stone tools remained the most commonly used tools throughout this period, known as the Copper Age, or Chalcolithic (Copper-Stone) Age.

Rib bones of a skeleton from Varna

◄ COPPER ORE
Copper is mostly found mixed with other minerals, as an ore, which is easy to recognize thanks to its bright color. This is malachite, a green copper ore. From around 5000 BCE, people in Afghanistan, Iran, the Balkans, and Spain were collecting ores and heating them to extract copper. They would place a lump like this in a kiln (furnace), and the pure red metal would flow out. This technique is called smelting.

COPPER TOOLS ►
Melted copper was poured into molds to make tools such as this adze, a tool used to shape wood. Across Europe, copper tools became so fashionable that there was a new demand for copper-colored flint axes, from Grand Pressigny in western France. To see how effective such tools were, archaeologists used both a copper and a modern steel ax to cut down yew trees. While the steel ax did the job in 15 minutes, it took 45 minutes with the copper ax.

THE ICE MAN

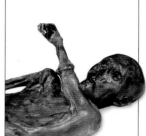

ÖTZI DISCOVERED
In 1991, hikers in the Ötztal Alps between Austria and Italy found the body of a man. Thinking he had died recently, they called the police. From the man's strange belongings, which included flint-headed arrows, it became clear that he was very old indeed. The dead man, nicknamed Ötzi, lived 5,300 years ago.

ÖTZI RECONSTRUCTED
This reconstruction shows Ötzi as he would have appeared in life. He was well-equipped for survival in the snow-covered Alps. Beneath a grass cape, which could be used as a blanket at night, he wore layers of warm clothing made from goat and deer hide. His hat was bearskin and his deer hide shoes were stuffed with grass. Other equipment included a wooden-framed backpack, a bow with 14 arrows, a flint-bladed dagger, a copper ax, and berries for food. At his feet stand two bark containers, one holding charcoal for fire.

YEW HANDLE

AX BLADE

COPPER AX ▲
Ötzi's most prized possession was this ax. The copper blade was bound to the wooden handle with leather thongs. The handle is 2 ft (60 cm) long and made of yew. This is the only complete prehistoric ax ever found. Tests revealed that the copper had been obtained locally. Ötzi also had copper particles in his hair, and it is possible that he was a coppersmith by profession.

▲ RICH GRAVES
Before the Copper Age, the most valuable objects were polished stone axes. Copper and gold—scarce and attractive metals—were a new form of wealth that was easy to carry around. Trade links spread across Europe, and some people became very rich. The wealth of this period can be seen at the Varna cemetery in Bulgaria, where there are graves containing the world's oldest gold ornaments. This skeleton from Varna, covered with gold and copper jewelry, dates from between 4000 and 3500 BCE.

copper

BRONZE-AGE EUROPE

Around 3500 BCE, metalworkers in Anatolia (now Turkey) discovered that they could make copper harder by mixing it with a small amount of tin. The tin stops copper crystals from sliding over each other. This new metal, 90 percent copper and 10 percent tin, is called bronze, and it gives its name to the next period of prehistory. The Bronze Age began in Europe around 2000 BCE, and lasted until about 900 BCE. In Europe, tin (a rare metal) is found in Brittany in France, Cornwall in England, northern Italy, and southern Spain. The demand for tin was a huge boost to trade, which created a rich aristocracy.

▲ COPPER MINE
With the invention of bronze, both copper and tin were mined on a huge scale. The world's largest Bronze-Age copper mine is at Great Orme, in Wales, where tunnels stretch 230 ft (70 m). Some are so small that they must have been made by children.

◀ HAMMER STONE
The miners at Great Orme used lumps of hard volcanic stone, called diabase, as hammers. They collected these from the nearby beaches, and used them to pound the walls of the mine, detaching lumps of copper ore. They also lit fires against the rock face to make it crack. From 1900 to 900 BCE, some 1,940 tons (1,770 metric tons) of copper were mined here.

MOLDS ▶
Molten copper and tin were mixed and then poured into molds to make bronze swords, daggers, spear heads, and axes. This is a simple open mold, carved from stone, for two axes of different sizes. Molds were also made of clay. These were in two parts which were fitted together. The advantage of a two-part mold was that it could be used to make axes with curved sides to form an edge.

◀ BRONZE AX
This bronze ax was made in a clay mold. Its right end is flattened, with a rectangular rim called a "flange," for attaching the blade to its wooden handle. This was a much more effective tool than a copper ax because the edge did not need constant sharpening. The amount of copper mined at Great Orme was enough to make 10 million bronze axes like this.

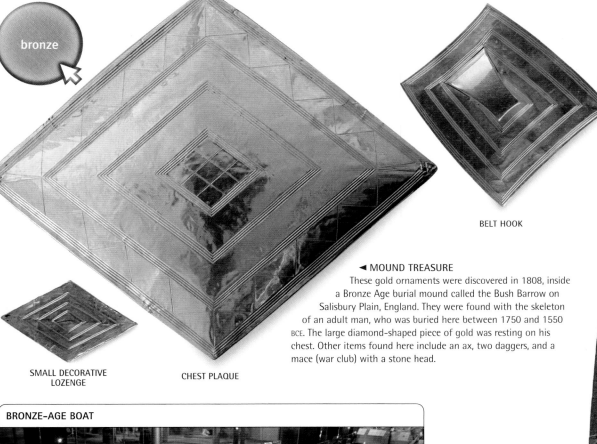

◄ BURIAL MOUNDS

Each period of prehistory brought new ways of burying the dead. The Bronze-Age people built burial mounds, which were graves for rich and powerful individuals. Mounds were often placed on hilltops, so that they could be seen for miles around. The dead were buried inside with many precious items. Some of the richest Bronze-Age graves are found in northwest France and southwest England, which both controlled tin sources.

bronze

BELT HOOK

◄ MOUND TREASURE

These gold ornaments were discovered in 1808, inside a Bronze Age burial mound called the Bush Barrow on Salisbury Plain, England. They were found with the skeleton of an adult man, who was buried here between 1750 and 1550 BCE. The large diamond-shaped piece of gold was resting on his chest. Other items found here include an ax, two daggers, and a mace (war club) with a stone head.

SMALL DECORATIVE LOZENGE

CHEST PLAQUE

BRONZE-AGE BOAT

Boats were used to transport copper, tin, and finished bronze artifacts. This Bronze-Age vessel was found by workers digging a hole in Dover, England, in 1992. Built 3,500 years ago, it is the world's oldest known seaworthy boat. It could easily have been rowed across the English Channel to France, carrying up to 3 tons of cargo. It was made of oak planks sewn together with lengths of twisted yew. Nails were not invented until the Iron Age.

BRONZE SHEATH ►

Bronze was also beaten into sheets, and bent with a hammer to make helmets, cauldrons, and sheaths for swords and daggers. This sheath, found in the Thames River, England, was made of a dozen small strips of sheet bronze, which were riveted together. Many precious bronze objects like this were found in rivers and pools, where they were placed as offerings to the gods or the spirits of the dead.

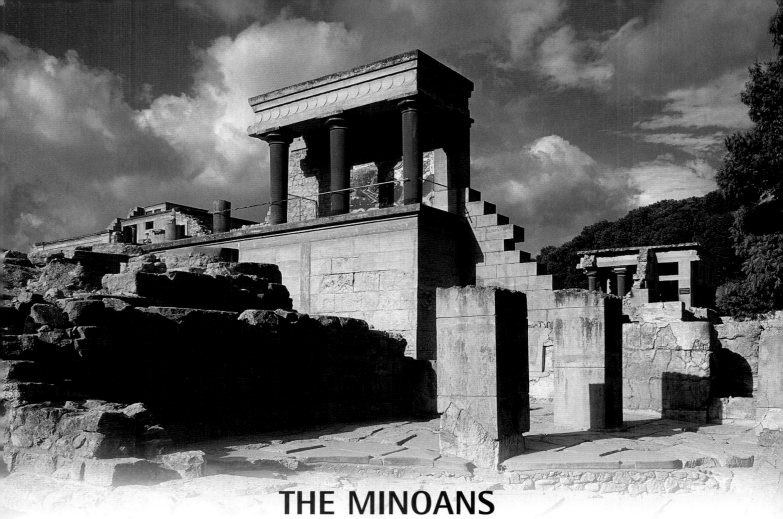

THE MINOANS

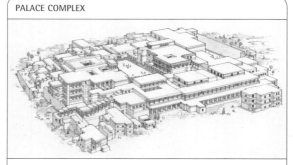

▲ KNOSSOS RESTORED
This is the palace of Knossos, excavated by Arthur Evans. He rebuilt part of the palace to show how he believed the upper levels would have looked. Evans based these painted colonnades on Minoan paintings of columns, which were made of wood and have not survived. Many of the walls were covered with beautiful paintings, which he found as tiny fragments of colored plaster. Putting them together was like working a jigsaw puzzle with half the pieces missing.

Between 1900 and 1903, English archaeologist Arthur Evans (1851–1941) uncovered a vast palace, built by a previously unknown Bronze-Age civilization, at Knossos on the island of Crete in the eastern Mediterranean. He called its people "Minoans," after Minos, a legendary king of Crete. Soon, more palaces were found at Malia, Phaestos, and Zakros. None of them had any defensive walls—either the Minoans were not warlike, or they had a powerful fleet to defend their island from attack. Their civilization, the oldest in Europe, was at its height between 2000 and 1500 BCE.

PALACE COMPLEX

The Knossos palace was a vast complex, covering 140,000 sq ft (13,000 sq m) and containing 1,300 rooms. More than just a palace, it was also a religious center and a seat of government. It had storage areas, where olive oil, grain, dried fish, beans, and wine were kept in large clay jars. There were workshops, used by craftworkers, such as potters, weavers, and metalworkers. The palace had an advanced plumbing system, with drains and flushing toilets.

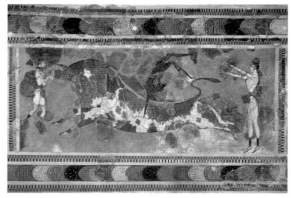

◄ THE BULL LEAPERS
A restored wall painting from Knossos shows young Minoans leaping over the back of a bull, in what may be a sport or a religious ritual. Bulls seem to have been sacred to the Minoans and often appear in their art. The Minoan bull cult may be the origin of the later Greek legend of the Minotaur—a monster, half man and half bull, that lived at Knossos.

OBJECTS OF WORSHIP

SNAKE GODDESS
At Knossos, Evans found a clay statuette of a woman gripping two snakes, with a cat sitting on her head. These animals suggest that the figurine is of a goddess. The multilayered dress shows the elaborate clothing worn by wealthy Minoan women.

SANCTUARIES
Minoans worshipped their gods in sacred caves and at open-air sanctuaries on mountain peaks. Here they left behind offerings such as clay figurines of gods, worshippers, and animals. This figurine, wearing a tall hat, is of a goddess.

◄ THERA
Traces of the Minoan civilization have been found beyond Crete. This wall painting, from the island of Thera (now Santorini), is in Minoan style, showing Cretan architecture and dress. The people of Thera may have been settlers from Crete, or locals who copied the Minoan way of life. The painting shows a small ship being rowed past a palace, where people watch from the upper walls.

▲ KEEPING RECORDS
The Minoans invented a writing system, called Linear A, to keep records. This has not been deciphered, and we do not know what language they spoke. This script was later adapted by the Greeks, who took over Knossos around 1450 BCE. The tablet above shows the Greek script, Linear B. Each upright line stands for the number one.

Minoans

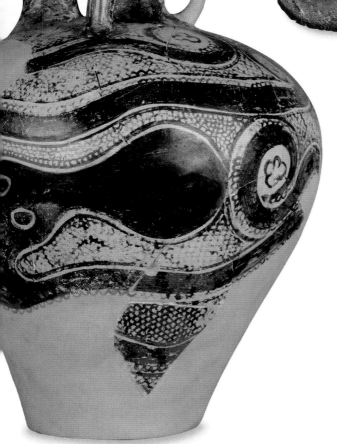

▲ OCTOPUS POT
Minoan potters made beautiful vessels, often decorated with paintings of sea creatures, including starfish, sea urchins, dolphins, and octopuses. Pots, such as this vase, have been found in Egypt, Greece, and Syria, and are proof of long-range trade. The Minoans exported pottery, lumber, and olive oil, and imported ivory, tin, silver, and gold. These were the raw materials they needed for their craft workshops.

▲ END OF THE MINOANS
Around 1450 BCE, most of the palaces, including Phaestos (above), were destroyed. Minoan towns were also abandoned, for unknown reasons. Only Knossos was spared. It was reoccupied by the Greeks, who may have destroyed the other palaces, or may simply have taken advantage of the fall of Minoan civilization. Greeks ruled at Knossos until around 1380 BCE, when it too was finally destroyed and abandoned. The Minoans would be forgotten for more than 3,000 years.

MYCENAE

The Minoans were a great influence on the people of mainland Greece, who, in the Bronze Age, are called Mycenaeans, after Mycenae, their most important town. The Mycenaeans copied Minoan fashions, pottery, and wall paintings. Yet they were much more warlike than the Minoans. Their palaces were heavily fortified, and their men were buried with arms and armor. By the 14th century BCE, the Mycenaeans were the leading power in the eastern Mediterranean.

▲ PALACE
The Mycenaeans lived in several kingdoms, each ruled from a palace, such as at Pylos, Mycenae, Tyrins, and Thebes. Each palace had a central hall, or megaron, where the wanax (king) held court, sitting on his throne. This is the brightly painted courtyard of the palace at Pylos, with the door to the megaron on the left.

ROYAL GOLD ►
Mycenaean kings were very wealthy and were buried with vast amounts of gold. This is the so-called "mask of Agamemnon," named after a legendary king of Mycenae. It was found in 1876 by German archaeologist Heinrich Schliemann (1822–1890), who had gone to Mycenae to try to prove that Agamemnon really existed. It dates from around 1550 BCE.

▲ FORTIFICATIONS
Mycenaean palaces are much smaller than Minoan ones, yet far more work went into fortifying them. Their massive walls, such as this one at Tiryns, were up to 23 ft (7 m) thick. The need to build such fortifications shows that warfare was common. Later, the Greeks called such walls "Cyclopean" because they thought that they were built by one-eyed giants called Cyclopes.

▲ THE LION GATE
The entrance to the palace at Mycenae, the Lion Gate, is the oldest monumental sculpture in Europe. It has a triangular limestone slab carved with two lions on either side of a pillar, an image that also appears on Mycenaean seals. This may have been the royal coat of arms, or lions may have been sacred to the Mycenaeans. The lintel stone below the lions is 15 ft (4.5 m) long and weighs about 20 tons (18 metric tons).

▲ HUNTING LIONS

This bronze dagger is decorated with gold-and-silver figures showing a favorite Mycenaean pastime—hunting. Young men can be seen hunting lions with spears and bows, protected by long shields. These were the same weapons used in warfare, so hunting also served as military training. Hunting was a dangerous sport—one of the hunters has fallen beneath the feet of the charging lion. During Mycenaean times, wild lions could still be found in Greece.

DETAIL OF A CHARGING LION

Tusks in rows, facing in alternating directions

TUSK HELMET ▲

Mycenaeans hunted wild boar for their meat and their tusks, which were sewn on to leather backings to make helmets. Since they are very hard, the tusks offered good protection in battle. The helmets were considered particularly appropriate for warfare, because the boar was regarded as an aggressive fighter. They were also a mark of high status, since it took 30 to 40 animals to make each one.

Mycenae

OFF TO BATTLE ▶

Warfare is a frequent subject in Mycenaean art. This detail is from a "warrior vase" found by Heinrich Schliemann at Mycenae. It shows an army marching off to battle, carrying shields and spears. Unlike noble Mycenaeans, who wore boars'-tusk helmets and rode to battle in chariots, these are ordinary foot soldiers. They wear helmets decorated with plumes and horns. The white dots on their clothing may be bronze disks, sewn on to the leather for protection. Small bags hang from the men's spears, perhaps containing the day's rations.

THE COMING OF IRON

The most common metal on Earth is iron, yet this was the last to be worked. Iron smelting required much higher temperatures than copper or tin, and new techniques were needed. These were first developed in the Middle East, some time after 1550 BCE. Ironworking gradually spread westward, reaching Britain by 700 BCE. Iron was harder than copper, readily available, and changed ordinary people's lives across Europe, Asia, and Africa. It was used to make weapons, tools, cooking pots, horse harnesses, and nails. Bronze became a metal used mostly for ornaments.

◄ IRON FROM METEORITES
Pure iron has always been available in small amounts, from meteorites—rocks from space that hit earth. The Egyptians called this "black copper from the sky," and valued it even more than gold. Around 1340 BCE, Pharaoh Tutankhamun was buried with two daggers (left), one with an iron blade carved from meteorite, and one made of gold.

| GOLD SCABBARD | IRON DAGGER | GOLD DAGGER | GOLD SCABBARD | METEORITE |

IRON SMELTING

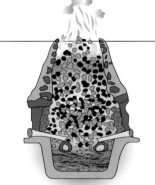

IRON ORE
The first stage in smelting was to collect iron ore—rocks containing iron, recognizable by their reddish color. This is caused by iron oxide, or rust, formed when iron combines with oxygen. To obtain usable metal, the oxygen must be removed by heating the ore with charcoal.

FURNACE
The ore is placed with burning charcoal in a clay furnace. Two bellows (not shown) are used to pump in air at the bottom. The amount of oxygen is carefully controlled. Too much can stop the smelting process. Too little will prevent the charcoal from getting hot enough.

BLOOM
The burning charcoal gives off carbon monoxide, which combines with the oxygen from the ore. As the iron loses its oxygen content, it is reduced to metal. After several hours, the reduced iron forms a bloom—a spongy mass at the bottom of the furnace.

USABLE IRON
The bloom still contains impurities. These are removed by repeatedly heating and hammering the iron. This makes the melted impurities burst out. Eventually, a usable lump of iron metal is left. The lump shown above has been beaten until it is almost flat.

◄ AT THE FORGE
Unlike bronze, iron was not cast in a mold, but "forged," or hammered into shape.
The smith (metalworker) first heated the piece of iron on a bed of charcoal until it glowed a yellow-orange color, indicating that it was the right temperature for forging. Here, a smith holds a piece of hot iron with tongs.

◄ HAMMER AND ANVIL
Next, the smith beat the hot iron with a hammer over a large block called an anvil. He struck it with regular blows, forming the long shape of a sword. Smiths call this "drawing out." When the metal cooled down, it was reheated before being beaten again.
The word "smith" comes from "smite," an old English word meaning "hit."

Iron sword blade

iron

Iron hammer heads, as used by smiths

Iron spear points

Socket *for mounting on wooden shaft*

▲ NEW WEAPONS
Iron technology made it cheap and easy to produce weapons like these spear heads and sword. As a result, warfare became much more common in the Iron Age than the earlier Bronze Age. Across Europe, new types of fortifications were built because people needed to defend themselves from attack.

▲ HILLFORT
In southern Britain, the Iron Age saw the building of great hillforts, protected by ditches and embankments. This one, called Maiden Castle, was built in Dorset between 450 and 300 BCE. The entrance to the hillfort, at bottom right, is defended by a maze of ditches and banks.

▲ ROUNDHOUSE
Maiden Castle would have been filled with thatched roundhouses, like this modern reconstruction. It is based on an Iron-Age house found at Longbridge Deverel Cowdown in Wiltshire, England. It is 50 ft (15 m) in diameter and has 16 tons (15 metric tons) of thatch on the roof. This would have been home to a powerful chieftain.

▲ BROCH
Scotland had its own style of Iron-Age fortification, with around 500 stone towers called brochs. Experts argue whether these served mainly as military strongholds or to display wealth and power. They stand up to 43 ft (13 m) high and have walls 10 ft (3 m) thick.

THE FIRST AMERICAN FARMERS

From around 8000 BCE, soon after farming was invented in the Middle East, people in the Americas also began to grow crops and domesticate animals. The plants and animals raised were very different here. In Mesoamerica (middle America), the main crops were corn, squash, beans, tomatoes, and peppers. Corn, which could grow almost anywhere, soon spread to South America, where people also cultivated beans, peppers, squash, quinoa, and potatoes. However, there were few animals that could be domesticated. In South America there was just the llama, the alpaca, and the guinea pig, and in Mesoamerica only the turkey. The Muscovy duck was found in both areas. Yet farming was able to support 25 times as many people as hunting and gathering.

EARLY FARMING AREAS

ATLANTIC OCEAN

MESOAMERICA

PACIFIC OCEAN

SOUTH AMERICA

This map shows in green the areas where crops and animals were first domesticated. Evidence comes from finds of early crops, such as corn, preserved in dry caves and from the present-day location of wild ancestors of domesticated crops.

CORN DOMESTICATION

TEOSINTE
Corn was domesticated from a wild grass called teosinte. Its ear is 2–3 in (5–7 cm) long, with up to 12 small kernels, each encased in a hard coating. Teosinte is so different from corn that 19th-century botanists did not think the two plants could be related.

THE CHANGE TO CORN
As a result of farmers repeatedly planting seeds from only the best plants, teosinte kernels became bigger and softer and lost their hard coating. They grew in multiple rows, forming a cob, which stayed on the plant until it was harvested. A corn cob can be up to 12 in (30 cm) long, with 500 kernels.

COOKING CORN
The cobs were soaked in water and ash. Although this was done to remove the soft outer husk, the ash also increased the protein and vitamin content. It was then ground into flour on a grinding-stone (above), shaped into pancakes called tortillas, and cooked on a stone or clay griddle.

◄ **BEANS**
Many varieties of wild bean were domesticated and farmed in both Mesoamerica and South America. The plants changed as a result of people gathering pods that had not split apart. Eventually, the plant evolved so that the beans remained in their pods until they were picked. This meant that, like corn, beans could no longer survive without humans to plant them. Beans were perfect to grow alongside corn because they fix nitrogen in the soil, which provides nutrients for the corn.

LIMA BEANS

◄ **CHILI PEPPERS**
There are many varieties of chili. These were domesticated at different times in different places, from around 4000 BCE. Domesticated chilies had bigger fruit than their wild ancestors. Chilies are a rich source of vitamins A and C, but people grew them because they loved the hot flavor they gave to food.

◄ BEES

In Mesoamerica, people kept stingless bees for honey, which they used to sweeten food and as medicine. The bees build nests in hollow logs, which Mesoamerican people would cut to a manageable size and hang from the walls of their houses. The insects also served the useful purpose of pollinating crops.

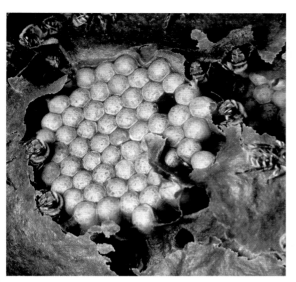

▲ GUINEA PIGS

Native to the valleys of the Andes, guinea pigs were domesticated as an important meat source. Though small, they have more meat than other rodents, which may be the result of selective breeding. They have a high reproductive rate and can thrive in small spaces, making them easy to rear and keep.

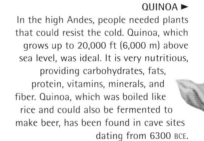

▼ LLAMAS AND ALPACAS

In the Andes mountains of South America, people domesticated llamas and alpacas (below) for meat and hide. Later they were kept for their wool and as pack animals. They also provided fat for burning lamps and dung for fuel and fertilizer. Llamas can carry loads of up to 130 lb (60 kg), but are not strong enough to pull carts. The wheel was not used in early America, except for pull-along toys.

QUINOA ►

In the high Andes, people needed plants that could resist the cold. Quinoa, which grows up to 20,000 ft (6,000 m) above sea level, was ideal. It is very nutritious, providing carbohydrates, fats, protein, vitamins, minerals, and fiber. Quinoa, which was boiled like rice and could also be fermented to make beer, has been found in cave sites dating from 6300 BCE.

▲ MUSCOVY DUCKS

Despite being named after the Russian capital, Moscow, the Muscovy duck is native to the Americas. It was domesticated in both Mesoamerica and South America. It is larger than most ducks, making it a good source of meat. Originally a forest species, it is the only duck that likes to roost in trees.

farmers

PUEBLO AND MOUND-BUILDERS

From 700 CE, the first large towns were built in North America. In the eastern woodlands, people created large towns around the Mississippi River valley. Filled with rectangular, flat-topped earth mounds and grouped around open plazas, they were ceremonial and administrative centers that organized the production and distribution of food and manufactured goods. Meanwhile, in the dry southwest, farmers called the Anasazi built large villages as single structures, crowded with rooms. These are called "pueblos," Spanish for towns or villages, and the Anasazi are also known as the pueblo people. Although the mound builders and Anasazi were very different, their societies were both based on farming, with main crops of corn, beans, and squash.

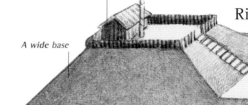

Chief or council chamber

A wide base

▲ MONK'S MOUND
This is the Monk's Mound in Cahokia, today in the state of Illinois, where the Mississippi, Missouri, and Illinois rivers meet. The mound is over 100 ft (30 m) high, with a base bigger than the largest Egyptian pyramid. Unlike an Egyptian pyramid, it was made wholly of earth. The wooden building on top may have served as the home of the chief or as a council chamber. This is just one of the 100 mounds in Cahokia.

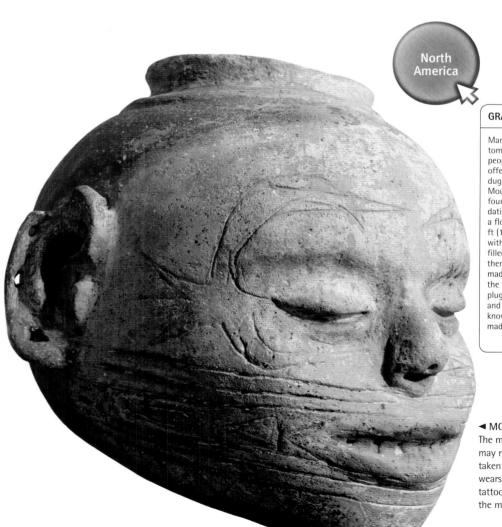

North America

GRAVE GOODS

Many mounds served as tombs, where important people were buried with offerings. Archaeologists dug into the Craig Mound in Oklahoma and found a large burial area, dating from 1400 CE, with a floor that was 37 by 55 ft (11 by 17 m). It was covered with human bones and baskets filled with grave goods. Among them was this mask with deer antlers, made of red cedar wood, inset with shell for the eyes and teeth. The ears were pierced for large plugs. Similar objects have been found in mounds across the southeast, and they have been interpreted as evidence of a widespread religion, known as the Southern Cult. Another idea is that they were artifacts made in places like Cahokia that were then traded.

◄ MOUND-BUILDER POTTERY
The mound-builders made pots in the form of human heads, which may represent ancestors or even trophies—the heads of enemies taken in war. The head has closed eyes, a sign that he is dead. He wears large round plugs in his ears, and the lines on his face suggest tattooing, decorative scarring, or face paint. This pot shows what the mound-builders themselves may have looked like.

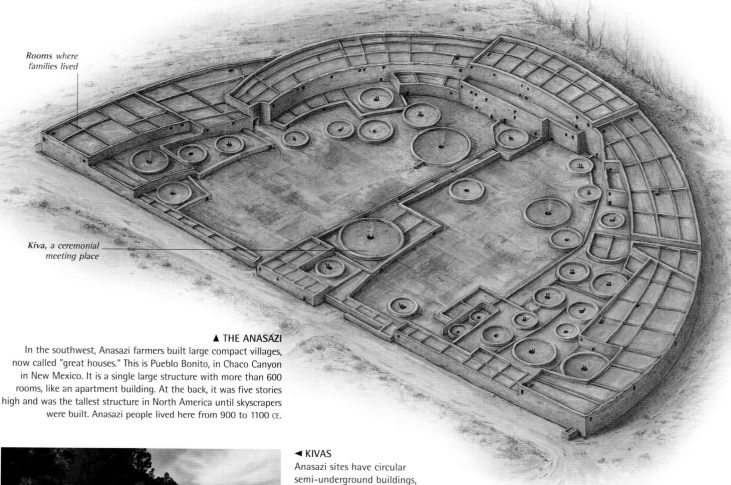

Rooms where families lived

Kiva, a ceremonial meeting place

▲ THE ANASAZI

In the southwest, Anasazi farmers built large compact villages, now called "great houses." This is Pueblo Bonito, in Chaco Canyon in New Mexico. It is a single large structure with more than 600 rooms, like an apartment building. At the back, it was five stories high and was the tallest structure in North America until skyscrapers were built. Anasazi people lived here from 900 to 1100 CE.

◄ KIVAS

Anasazi sites have circular semi-underground buildings, known as kivas. Their large size, up to 65 ft (20 m) across, suggests they were public meeting places rather than houses. People may have gathered here to hold ceremonies to bring rain, luck in hunting, or a good harvest. Each kiva was covered with a timber roof covered with mud, with an opening in the middle. People entered by climbing down a ladder from the roof.

◄ CLIFF PALACE

Around 1200, the Anasazi abandoned their villages on the floor of Chaco Canyon, and built a new, better-protected settlement, known as the Cliff Palace, high in a canyon wall. They climbed up using hand and toe holes cut into the rock face. Soon after 1300, the Cliff Palace was abandoned too. Tree rings from timbers here show that there was a 22-year drought, between 1276 and 1299. This disaster may explain the abandonment of the Cliff Palace.

PACK-RAT MIDDENS

Archaeologists learned about the end of the Anasazi by studying the nests or middens (garbage dumps) of pack rats. Generations of rats nest in the same place, bringing in twigs from an area within 150 ft (50 m) of the nest. These nests, which can be carbon-dated, reveal what local vegetation was like in Anasazi times. They show that the Anasazi cut down all the trees around their settlements for building lumber and fuel. Toward the end, they had to travel 75 miles (120 km) to gather wood.

MESOAMERICA

Mesoamerica (middle America) is the name for the region that stretches from central Mexico in the north, down to Guatemala in the south. It was here that the earliest civilizations of America developed. Across Mesoamerica, different people came in contact with each other, and their civilizations came to share many features. They were ruled by kings, built towns with pyramid temples, worshipped similar gods, and played the same ballgame. From an early date, warfare was a way of life, and prisoners were often sacrificed to gods.

▲ OLMECS
The first Mesoamerican civilization was that of the Olmecs, who lived in the tropical jungles on the north coast of Mexico, between 1200 and 300 BCE. They built temple complexes made of earth and clay, so little remains of their buildings. With no stone available locally, the Olmecs had to import basalt rocks from the mountains, which they used for carving colossal heads of their rulers.

▲ THE BALLGAME
All Mesoamerican people played a ballgame in specially built courts. The players controlled a heavy rubber ball by striking it with their elbows and hips. The game at times represented the movement of heavenly bodies, or a reenactment of warfare, or myths. The ballcourt shown above is at Monte Alban in Mexico, the capital of the Zapotecs, who lived to the south of the Olmecs.

◄ WERE-JAGUAR
Olmec carvings show strange-looking humans with downturned, fleshy mouths and clefts (splits) along the top of their heads. They are called "were-jaguars," since the cleft is a feature of male jaguars. Some experts believe that the face is really meant to represent a toad. This youth holds a "were-jaguar" baby who must be some kind of supernatural being.

◄ THE ZAPOTECS
The oldest surviving city in the Americas is the Zapotec capital, Monte Alban, established near the south coast around 500 BCE. It contains hundreds of stone carvings, made between 350 and 200 BCE, showing life-sized figures called *Los Danzantes* (the dancers) because of their postures. However, they are not dancers, but dead prisoners. Each figure has a picture sign, which may stand for a town captured by the Zapotecs.

▲ TEOTIHUACÁN

The most spectacular Mesoamerican site is Teotihuacán in Mexico, which lasted from c. 150 BCE to c. 750 CE. At its peak in 500 CE, it was the sixth-largest city in the world with a population of 200,000. It was a planned city, built to a grid design, with a grand central avenue lined with 75 temples. The temple shown above is the Pyramid of the Sun, which is 246 ft (75 m) high.

CRAFTS ►

Archaeologists have identified more than 600 craft workshops in Teotihuacán, where people made pottery and ornaments from precious stones, shells, and colorful feathers. Goods produced here have been found all over Mesoamerica. This is a stone mask decorated with tiles of blue turquoise and red seashells. It was probably attached to a wooden statue, dressed in textiles and feathers, which represented an ancestor or a god.

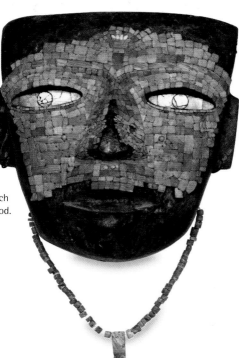

Mesoamerica

▲ NECKLACE OF TEETH

Like other Mesoamericans, the people of Teotihuacán were warriors who conquered an empire in Mexico and captured prisoners for sacrifice. Inside the temple of the Feathered Serpent god (left), archaeologists found the skeletons of 200 warriors. One warrior, whose skull can be seen above, was buried here wearing necklaces strung with 136 human teeth and seven jawbones.

◄ FEATHERED SERPENT

In Teotihuacán, people worshipped gods, who would continue to be important in Mesoamerica for many hundreds of years. This carving from Teotihuacán shows one god in the form of a rattlesnake with bird's feathers. He was also worshipped by the Olmecs, the Maya, and the later Aztecs of Mexico. In Teotihuacán wall paintings, he is accompanied by drops of rain, suggesting that he was originally a water god. For the Aztecs, who called him Quetzalcoatl, he was the wind god who brought the rain clouds across the sky. It is not known what the people of Teotihuacán called him.

THE MAYA

Deep in the rainforests of Central America are the ruins of ancient cities, built between 200 and 900 CE by a people called the Maya. Without the use of metal tools, they built tall pyramids and palaces. The Maya were skilled artists, and made beautiful sculptures and wall paintings. They were experts at astronomy and mathematics, compiling calendars based on the sun, moon, and planets. They were also the only people in the Americas to invent a full writing system.

LAND OF THE MAYA

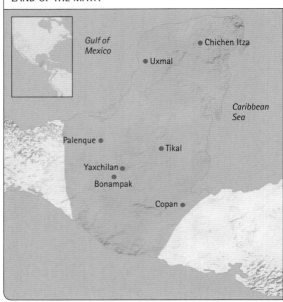

Gulf of Mexico

Chichen Itza

Uxmal

Caribbean Sea

Palenque

Tikal

Yaxchilan

Bonampak

Copan

The Mayan civilization (green) covered what is now Guatemala, Honduras, Belize, and southern Mexico. On the northern coast, the landscape is dry and scrubby, while the south is made up of highlands covered in pine forest. The rest of the territory is rainforest, where it rains heavily from May to October and is dry for the rest of the year. Here the Maya lived in many rival kingdoms, each based around a city that ruled the neighboring countryside. The Mayan civilization came to an end around 900 CE, when most cities were abandoned, for reasons that are still a mystery.

◄ TIKAL
The largest Mayan city was Tikal, once home to 50,000–100,000 people and covering 23 sq miles (60 sq km). Most of Tikal is now covered by jungle. Only the ceremonial area, with its pyramid temples, has been cleared. This temple, which is 144 ft (44 m) high, was for the worship of Kukulcan, the Mayan name for the Feathered Serpent god.

MAYAN KING ►
Each city was ruled by a king, who was both a chief priest and a war leader. His main role was to perform religious ceremonies. This carving, called a "stone tree," was set up by King 18 Rabbit of Copan. It depicts the king, together with descriptions of ceremonies he performed. King 18 Rabbit ruled Copan from 695 to 738 CE, when he was captured and sacrificed by the ruler of a rival city.

RITUAL BLOODLETTING

POWER OF BLOOD
Royal blood was believed to have great power. Kings and queens marked important occasions by drawing their blood, using stingray spines and ropes studded with thorns. In this carving, Lady Xoc, wife of King Shield Jaguar of Yaxchilan, is pulling a rope studded with thorns through her tongue. She collects the blood on rolled-up bark paper in the basket at her feet. Her husband holds a flaming torch, suggesting that this took place at night, or in the dark room of a temple.

VISION SERPENT
Bloodletting was thought to give Mayan rulers a way of speaking with their ancestors. In this carving, Lady Xoc (bottom right) has set the blood-soaked bark paper on fire. Out of the smoke has appeared a giant snake known as a "vision serpent." Its jaws open, and the figure of an ancestor who has become a god appears. These carvings record two separate bloodlettings. This one marks Shield Jaguar becoming king in 681 CE. The carving above is later, and celebrates the birth of Shield Jaguar's son, Bird Jaguar, in 709 CE.

BECOMING A GOD ▲
When kings died, they were often buried inside a pyramid, where their descendants would worship them as gods. One of the most successful rulers was Pacal of Palenque, who died in 683 CE, at the age of 80, after ruling for 68 years. Pacal was buried wearing this beautiful jade mask, the most precious material the Maya knew. The mask was found in many pieces, and carefully reconstructed.

Maya

▲ PRISONERS OF WAR
Mayan kings regularly went to war to capture high-ranking prisoners, often with their own hands. Captives were usually tortured and then sacrificed by beheading. In this wall painting from Bonampak, prisoners of war, who have had their fingernails torn out, are presented to a triumphant king called Chan Muwan (reigned 776–790 CE), who stands on the right. His finest warriors (top left) are distinguished by their elaborate headdresses.

EARLY SOUTH AMERICAN CIVILIZATIONS

Around 1200 BCE, when the Olmec people were creating the first civilization of Central America, the first South American civilization appeared in Peru, on the west coast of South America. It is called Chavin, after the famous site at Chavin de Huantar, and it laid the foundation for all later Peruvian civilizations. The Chavin dominated Peru until 500–300 BCE, when several regional cultures developed. In the north lived the warlike Moche, who made fine ceramics. In the south were the Paracas people, who made beautiful textiles, and the Nazca, who created mysterious pictures in the desert.

Peru

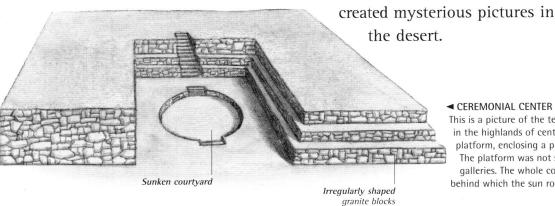
Sunken courtyard

Irregularly shaped granite blocks

◄ CEREMONIAL CENTER
This is a picture of the temple complex at Chavin de Huantar, in the highlands of central Peru. It has a U-shaped stone platform, enclosing a plaza with a sunken circular court. The platform was not solid, but filled with long, narrow galleries. The whole complex faced toward a pointed hill, behind which the sun rose on midsummer day.

▲ ROCK CARVINGS
Chavin de Huantar was filled with carvings of jaguars, eagles, and supernatural beings, such as this human with long fangs. The same style of sculpture has been found across Peru. This shows the widespread influence of the Chavin culture, but there is no evidence that there was a single state.

PARACAS MUMMIES

MUMMIES
Around 500 BCE, people in the Paracas peninsula on the southern coast of Peru began to preserve their dead as mummies. They placed a body in a squatting position, with knees drawn up to the chin, and wrapped it in many layers of textiles. The dry desert air stopped the bodies from decaying.

TEXTILES
The textiles used to wrap the mummies are the finest ever found in the Americas. Woven from cotton and alpaca wool on huge looms, they were embroidered with brightly colored patterns and pictures of strange animals. This figure may be dancing or flying through the air.

JEWELRY
Many of the dead wore jewelry such as gold disks and necklaces like this one. One mummy was buried with 56 items of clothing, including 13 turbans. There were 429 Paracas mummies, almost all elderly men. They must have been rich and important people.

▲ THE NAZCA SPIDER

Around 200 BCE, the Paracas were succeeded in southern Peru by the Nazca, who continued the practice of burying the dead as mummies. The Nazca also made vast drawings in the desert, by clearing away dark surface stones to reveal the lighter subsoil. The complete images, such as this 150-ft- (45-m-) long spider, can only be seen from the air, yet there are no hills nearby. The Nazca could only have imagined what the picture looked like.

LORD OF SIPAN ▶

Around 100 CE, another culture appeared in the Moche valley of northern Peru. This is a recreation of the tomb of a Moche ruler, which was discovered in 1987. The man in the middle, known as the Lord of Sipan, was buried with elaborate headdresses and ceremonial regalia. The other skeletons are of three women and a child.

THE MOCHE

A BOUND CAPTIVE

This Moche vase shows a captive, stripped of his clothing, with his arms tied behind his back. The Moche were warriors, who captured prisoners to humiliate and sacrifice them. Paintings on vases show Moche lords cutting prisoners' throats and drinking their blood.

MAN AND CAT

Moche vases also show strange scenes with people and animals, such as this man and cat, perhaps a puma. The cat may be embracing him or about to eat him. Other vases show people riding on giant fish. Such scenes may depict events from Moche myths.

DAILY LIFE

Moche vases also show all kinds of daily activity. Above, an old woman with a lined forehead carries a load on her back. Other vases show women weaving, cooking, and carrying children, and men trying on clothes, carrying weapons, and playing musical pipes.

PORTRAIT VASES

Many Moche vases are individual portraits of nobles, whose faces express different emotions. They are shown laughing, angry, or deep in thought. These were made in molds, and many portraits of the same person have been found. Some also show the same individual at different ages.

EMPIRES OF THE ANDES

From 1430 to 1527 CE, the Incas from the Peruvian Andes conquered a vast empire. It stretched 2,200 miles (3,500 km) down the west coast of South America and included 12 million people, speaking more than 20 languages. The Incas called their empire "Tihuantisuyu" (land of the four quarters). Their ruler, the "Sapa Inca" (Sole Lord), was believed to be a child of the sun, and was treated as a god. This was one of the most organized empires the world has ever seen. Although they had no writing, the Incas controlled the lives of all their people, making them work for a part of each year on labor projects—building roads, towns, and irrigation canals. The Incas could also organize and feed large armies, and send news quickly from one part of the empire to another via their well-built roads.

▲ CHIMU EMPIRE

The Incas learned much from the Chimu, an earlier civilization, who established the first Andean Empire on the north coast, around 1000 CE. The 40-ft- (12-m-) high mud-brick walls of the Chimu capital, Chan Chan (above), are decorated with carvings of fish, pelicans, foxes, and other creatures. Chan Chan occupied an area of 7¾ sq miles (20 sq km) and had a population of about 100,000.

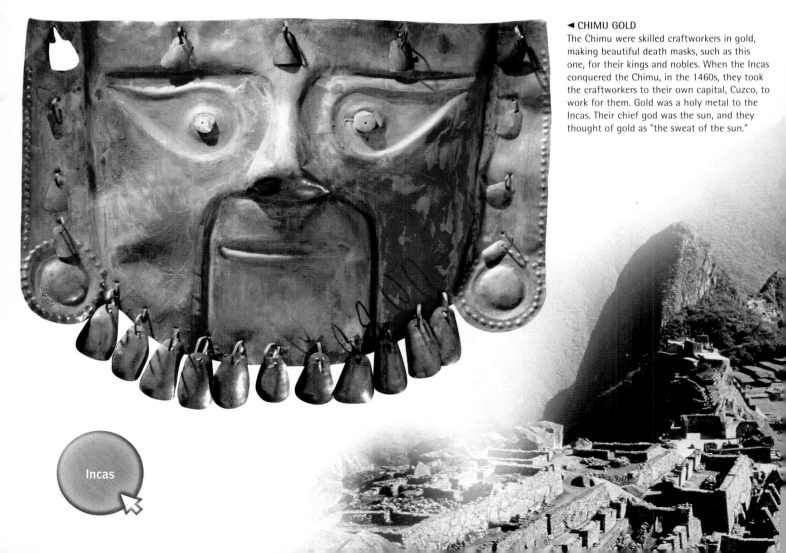

◄ CHIMU GOLD

The Chimu were skilled craftworkers in gold, making beautiful death masks, such as this one, for their kings and nobles. When the Incas conquered the Chimu, in the 1460s, they took the craftworkers to their own capital, Cuzco, to work for them. Gold was a holy metal to the Incas. Their chief god was the sun, and they thought of gold as "the sweat of the sun."

Incas

▲ INCA WALLS

The Incas built walls using huge, irregularly shaped stone blocks. Some of these blocks, from a fortress at Cuzco, the Inca capital, are 20 ft (6 m) high and weigh over 110 tons (100 metric tons). They are fitted together so precisely that it is impossible to slip a sheet of paper between them. The Inca walls had to be strong because earthquakes are common in Peru. In 1950, two-thirds of the modern city of Cuzco was destroyed by an earthquake, yet not one of the old walls fell.

▲ FARMING IN THE MOUNTAINS

Farmers grew crops, including corn, quinoa, and potatoes, on steep mountain slopes. They built stone-lined stepped terraces with flat surfaces that prevented rainwater from washing away the soil. For manure, they brought seagull dung up from the coast, using llamas as pack animals. They also maintained stone-lined irrigation channels bringing water from rivers. Above the terraces, the farmers built stone houses with straw-thatched roofs.

QUIPUS ►

Although the Inca did not invent a writing system, they kept records using lengths of knotted string called quipus. The color, number, and size of the knots, and the distance between them, all had a meaning. Quipus were used to record the past, though it is not known how much information they could carry.

◄ MACHU PICCHU

No other people on earth built towns as high up as the Incas. To help them cope with the low levels of oxygen at high altitude, the inhabitants evolved large lungs. This is Machu Picchu, which is 7,970 ft (2,430 m) above sea level. After the fall of the empire to Spanish conquerors, in the 1530s, Machu Picchu was the last Inca refuge. It was abandoned around 1550 and rediscovered in 1911.

ON THE MOVE
This is the Asian steppe, a grassy plain where nomads spent their lives on the move. They traveled with herds of cattle, sheep, and goats between summer pastures in the mountains and warmer lowland pastures in winter. They rode on horseback, pulling their belongings on carts. As nomads, they had no permanent homes, but lived in tents that they carried with them.

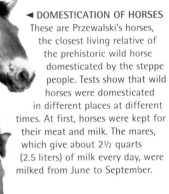

◄ DOMESTICATION OF HORSES
These are Przewalski's horses, the closest living relative of the prehistoric wild horse domesticated by the steppe people. Tests show that wild horses were domesticated in different places at different times. At first, horses were kept for their meat and milk. The mares, which give about 2½ quarts (2.5 liters) of milk every day, were milked from June to September.

THE BRIDLE ►
After keeping horses for meat and milk, the next stage was to ride them. A key invention for horse riding was the bridle. This fitted around the head with antler or bone fasteners, with a bar, called a bit, placed in the horse's mouth. By pulling on the reins connected to the bit, a rider could make a horse change direction, or stop in its tracks.

STEPPE NOMADS

The steppes of Europe and Asia are a vast, treeless plain, with icy winters and very hot summers. Although the region is not suitable for growing crops, it has grazing land for horses, cattle, sheep, and goats. Here, some time before 3000 BCE, people first learned to ride horses. Riding gave people their first fast mode of transportation and opened up the steppes to nomadic pastoralism, a way of life in which people on horseback led their animals to different places to look for fresh pastures.

WESTERN AND EASTERN STEPPES

EUROPE
Scythians
Black Sea
MONGOLIA   CHINA
Altai mountains
AFRICA

The steppes (shown in green) stretch for 3,000 miles (4,800 km), from the Carpathian mountains of Europe in the West to the borders of China in the East. To the south of the steppes were the lands of settled farming people, who were often raided by nomads.

TREASURES FROM THE KURGANS

GRIFFIN
This carving, made of gilded wood, was found in a Pazyryk kurgan. It is a 10½-in- (27-cm-) high head of a griffin, a mythical beast with the body of a lion and the head of an eagle. It has a deer's head in its mouth. This may have been an ornament worn by a horse, or it might have decorated a cart.

RIDER WITH A BOW
This felt hanging, which may have decorated the wall of a nomad's tent, shows a Pazyryk horseman with a short bow case near his leg. The bow was the main weapon used by nomads for war and hunting. It was short, so that it could be easily fired from the saddle, but very powerful, because it was made of sinew and bone.

STAG
This metal ornament, from a Scythian kurgan by the Black Sea, is a 2-in- (5.35-cm-) long model of a stag, shown resting on the ground, with its head folded back. Stags seem to have been sacred to the nomads, who were often tattooed with pictures of them. Nomads are even known to have made their horses wear false stag antlers.

▲ KURGANS
Since they were always on the move, nomads left few archaeological traces. However, we do have their kurgans—mounds where people were buried, along with their sacrificed horses. These kurgans are in the Pazyryk valley of the Altai mountains in central Asia. In the fifth century BCE, nomads would come here in summer to bury their dead. The soil froze in winter, preserving organic remains including human skin, clothing, and horse tack.

nomads

◄ SCYTHIAN GOLD
The richest kurgans were those of the Scythians, nomads who lived on the western steppes to the north of the Black Sea. These kurgans contain beautiful gold ornaments, including this figure of a rider. His pants, which protect the legs from rubbing against the horse's sides, were an invention of steppe nomads.

▲ TATTOOS
The nomads loved decorations, on both their belongings and their skin, which they covered with tattoos. This is the tattooed shoulder of a woman found in a Pazyryk kurgan. When discovered in 1933, she was nicknamed the "Ice Maiden." This tattoo shows a staglike creature, whose horns are turning into flowers. It was made by piercing the skin with a needle and rubbing soot into the wound.

ARCTIC PEOPLE

Humans are so adaptable that we have even managed to find a way of living in the cold Arctic. About 11,000 years ago, as the climate warmed, the northern ice sheets retreated and were replaced by tundra—a treeless landscape with low-lying vegetation, such as lichen and moss. This provided food for musk oxen and caribou (Arctic deer), which the hunter-gatherers followed north. By 2000 BCE, they had settled on the Arctic coasts and islands, where they hunted birds and deer, and caught fish. These first settlers made tiny stone blades, and their culture, which lasted until 800 BCE, is called the Arctic Small Tool Tradition. They were followed by two later prehistoric cultures, called the Dorset and the Thule.

CANADIAN ARCTIC

This illustrated map shows the Canadian Arctic, with Alaska at the top left and Greenland at the top right. The places inhabited by people are shaded red. The map also shows three snow houses, called igloos, two Thule hunters, and a selection of Arctic wildlife. There were almost no trees, and any driftwood washed ashore was eagerly seized to make sleds.

◄ THULE CULTURE
Around 1000 CE, a new people spread across the Arctic, from Alaska in the west. They are called the Thule, after a site in Greenland. Unlike the Dorset, the Thule took to the sea in boats made of skin to hunt whales and walruses. They were the ancestors of the modern Inuit (inhabitants of the Canadian Arctic and Greenland). This is a wooden Thule carving of a man.

▲ DORSET CULTURE
Named after a site on Baffin Island, Canada, the Dorset culture developed around 800 BCE. The Dorset hunted musk oxen and caribou on land, and seals and walruses from the shore or the edge of the sea ice. They made elaborately carved bone harpoons and needles, and carvings of birds and animals, such as this seal.

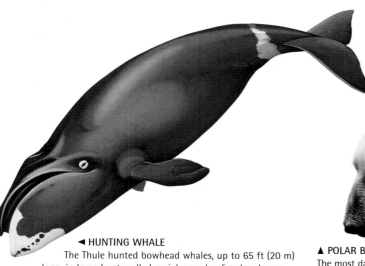

◄ HUNTING WHALE
The Thule hunted bowhead whales, up to 65 ft (20 m) long, in large boats called umiaks, made of walrus bones and covered with hides. They used harpoons with floats made of inflated sealskin attached to the lines, which prevented the whales from escaping by diving. One whale was enough to feed a village throughout winter.

▲ POLAR BEAR
The most dangerous animal hunted by the Thule was the polar bear, which can easily kill a human. Its fur was used to make warm clothing and its meat was eaten, apart from the liver, which contains poisonous levels of vitamin A. The liver had to be carefully thrown away, to stop the dogs from eating it.

◄ HUNTING SEAL

In winter, when the frozen sea ice made whaling impossible, hunters went after seals. They cut holes in the ice to provide breathing holes for the seals, which come up for air at regular intervals. This hunter is about to spear a seal with a toggling harpoon, which had a detachable head. Hunters might have had to wait hours for a seal to appear at a breathing hole.

THULE HOUSES

Throughout the winter, the Thule lived in houses with sunken floors, lined with stones, and walls made of whale bones covered with walrus hides. In this house, you can make out the white whale bones scattered among the darker stone slabs. In spring, when the snow melted and water leaked into the houses, people moved into tents made of skins. On hunting trips, they built temporary shelters, called igloos, out of snow blocks. These igloos do not survive, but we know that they were made because the Thule had special knives made of bone and horn for carving snow.

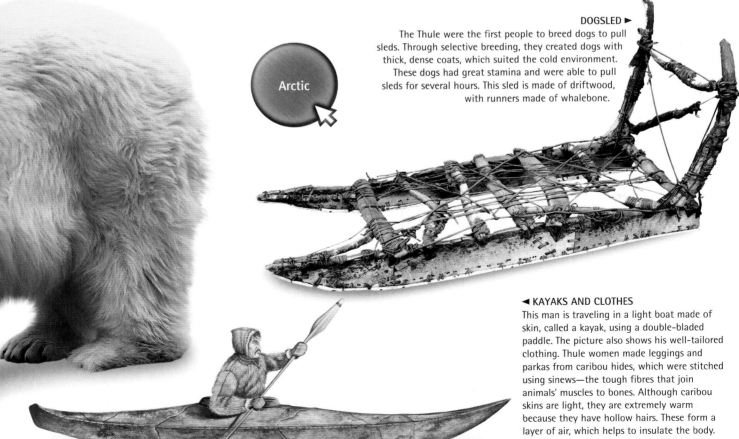

DOGSLED ►

The Thule were the first people to breed dogs to pull sleds. Through selective breeding, they created dogs with thick, dense coats, which suited the cold environment. These dogs had great stamina and were able to pull sleds for several hours. This sled is made of driftwood, with runners made of whalebone.

Arctic

◄ KAYAKS AND CLOTHES

This man is traveling in a light boat made of skin, called a kayak, using a double-bladed paddle. The picture also shows his well-tailored clothing. Thule women made leggings and parkas from caribou hides, which were stitched using sinews—the tough fibres that join animals' muscles to bones. Although caribou skins are light, they are extremely warm because they have hollow hairs. These form a layer of air, which helps to insulate the body.

PEOPLING THE PACIFIC

Polynesia (from the Greek for "many islands") is a vast triangular area in the Pacific Ocean, formed by New Zealand in the southwest, the Hawaiian islands in the north, and Easter Island in the southeast. It covers more than 8 million sq miles (20 million sq km), but less than one percent of this is land. By the 11th century CE, the widely scattered islands of Polynesia had been discovered and settled by a single race of people, speaking closely related languages.

▲ SAILING CANOE
The Polynesians made their voyages in large sailing canoes with twin hulls tied side by side. A 100-ft- (30-m-) long canoe could carry 100 passengers, as well as pigs, chickens, and dogs, plus a wide variety of plant seedlings, including coconut, taro, sweet potatoes, and breadfruit. The presence of plants and animals show that the Polynesian voyages were well-organized colonizing expeditions.

SETTLEMENT ROUTES

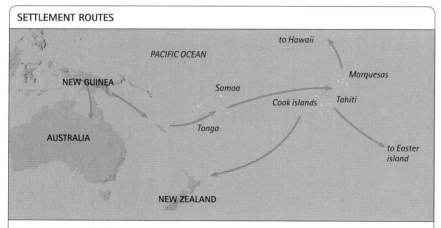

to Hawaii

PACIFIC OCEAN

NEW GUINEA

Samoa

Marquesas

Cook islands

Tahiti

Tonga

AUSTRALIA

to Easter island

NEW ZEALAND

The ancestors of the Polynesians came from southeast Asia, and moved down through New Guinea and out into the Pacific Ocean. By 1000 BCE, they had reached Tonga and Samoa. In the late first millennium BCE, the Polynesians began to explore the Pacific Ocean to their east, reaching the Marquesas by around 200 BCE. From the Marquesas, they went exploring in every direction. By the middle of the first millennium CE, they had reached Easter Island, Hawaii, Tahiti, and the Cook Islands. They went on to discover and settle New Zealand around the 11th century. New Zealand, called *Aeotearoa* (meaning "Land of the Long White Cloud") by the Polynesians, is larger than all the other islands put together. By the 11th century, the Polynesians were the most widespread people on Earth.

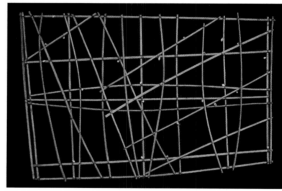

▲ FINDING THE WAY
At a time when European ships rarely spent more than a day or two out of sight of land, the Polynesians were making open-sea voyages of up to 3,000 miles (4,800 km), navigating with the aid of the sun and stars. This stick chart is a map, with islands as shells, and currents and winds represented by the sticks' angles.

THE MIGRATION OF ANIMALS

PIGS
The Polynesians took pigs with them to all the islands except New Zealand and Easter Island. Pigs were the perfect animals to take on voyages, since they feed on human waste. They were roasted over hot rocks in pits covered with leaves.

DOGS
Dogs were the second main source of meat for the Polynesians. Captain James Cook (1728–79), the British explorer, ate dog meat in Tahiti in 1769. He said that it tasted as good as English lamb, since the dogs were only fed vegetables.

CHICKENS
Chickens were carried everywhere except New Zealand. They were especially important on Easter Island, where the settlers had neither pigs nor dogs, and only sweet potatoes grew in the cooler climate.

RATS
Rats also accompanied the Polynesians, and reached almost every Pacific island. It is likely that they traveled as stowaways, not as a source of meat. Dozens of bird species became extinct after the arrival of rats in New Zealand.

◄ TATTOOED HEAD
"Tattoo" comes from the Polynesian word *tatau*, from Tahiti. The most spectacular tattoos were those of the Maori people of New Zealand. Using bone chisels, the Maoris made many small cuts in their skin, and then rubbed sooty coloring into the wounds. High-ranking Maoris used facial tattoos, called "Ta Moko," to display their status. The tattooed heads of dead chiefs (left) were preserved by their descendants.

EASTER ISLAND STATUES ►
Although the Polynesians had no pottery or metals, they were skilled at carving sculptures in stone and wood. Their sculptures often show gods and powerful ancestors. The largest of all are the 887 stone figures built on Easter Island between 1000 and 1600 CE. To make the rollers to transport the massive statues, the builders stripped Easter Island of its trees.

◄ WAR
This is a Polynesian war club, carved from hardwood. It was both an effective weapon and a symbol of high status. Warfare was common throughout Polynesia, as men fought to conquer territory and capture prisoners. After a battle, the victorious warriors often killed their prisoners and ate their roasted flesh. In the Marquesas, human flesh was a prized food, called "long pig."

Polynesians

◄ CHIEFS
This feathered collar was worn by a chief in Tahiti. Polynesians were ruled by chiefs, who claimed to be the descendants of the gods, with spiritual powers called "mana." To protect the power of the chiefs, many acts were considered "taboo" (forbidden). In Hawaii, people could not touch the clothes or shadows of their chiefs. In Tahiti, it was taboo even to mention their names. The penalty for breaking a taboo was death.

◄ GOOD LUCK
This is a "Hei Tiki," a carved greenstone pendant that the New Zealand Maori wore around their necks for luck. These were believed to possess magical power, which increased as they were passed on from generation to generation. The figure may represent the goddess of childbirth, a baby, or Tiki—the first man created by the gods, according to Maori legends.

TOWARD HISTORY

Prehistory came to an end when writing was invented or adopted. This happened in different places at different times. Writing was an invention of trading civilizations, such as the Egyptians, who needed to keep business records. The earliest texts are fragmentary, and often simply list goods. But within a few centuries after its invention, writing was used for letters, law codes, religious texts, and history. Reading these texts, we can hear people from the past speaking to us in their own words about their lives and beliefs.

▲ EGYPTIAN HIEROGLYPHS

Around 3300 BCE, the Egyptians invented a system of writing called hieroglyphs, or sacred signs. It used pictographs, or picture signs, which came to stand for sounds as well as words and ideas. So a picture of the sun stood for the word "sun," the ideas of "light" and "time," and the sound "r." This is the seal ring of the female pharaoh Hatshepsut, engraved with the hieroglyphs of her name and titles.

THE DEVELOPMENT OF CUNEIFORM

SUMERIAN WRITING
The second people to invent a writing system were the Sumerians, who lived in what is now southern Iraq. Their writing is called cuneiform ("wedge-shaped"). It was written on clay tablets like this. Sumerians made these signs by pressing a pointed reed, called a stylus, into the soft clay.

PICTOGRAPHS
The Sumerians first began by making picture signs, such as a cow's head (top left), a hand (top right), a foot (middle left), or wavy lines standing for water (right). Like Egyptian hieroglyphs, these picture signs came to stand for sounds, words, and ideas, as well as the objects shown.

CUNEIFORM
These signs were then simplified into a series of lines. On the left are the picture signs—a fish, a bird, a tree, and a cow's head. In the middle, the same signs are drawn as wedges. On the right, these have been so simplified that they no longer look like pictures. Cuneiform was invented around 3100 BCE.

CHINESE WRITING ▶

The Chinese script began as picture signs, which were simplified into lines for quick painting with a brush. Every sign stands for an object or idea, and there are no sound signs. The advantage of a writing system that is not based on sounds is that it can be read by people who speak different languages. Chinese people speak five different languages, but can all read the same newspapers. This Buddhist prayer book is 1,000 years old, yet any Chinese reader could read it today. The problem is, every new invention needs a new sign. To read a Chinese newspaper you need to know 4,000 signs, but there are more than 60,000 in all.

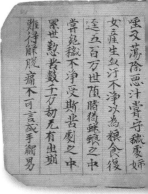

THE FIRST ALPHABET ▶
Our alphabet comes from the Phoenicians, a seafaring people living in the eastern Mediterranean, who started to write around 1600 BCE. They copied Egyptian hieroglyphs, but only made signs for consonants and vowels. So an ox-head sign, called "aleph" in Phoenician, stood for "a." The sign for a house, called "beth," represented the sound "b." The Greeks and Romans adopted this system and passed it on to us. The advantage of an alphabet is that there are few signs to learn.

ORACLE BONES ▶
Early writing has only survived when it appears on materials that do not perish, such as clay or stone. The earliest Chinese writing we have is from oracle bones dating back to 2500 BCE. These were questions written on turtle shells or ox shoulder blades (right), which were then burned. The resulting cracks were used to look into the future, and the interpretation was written on the bone. But Chinese writing was fully developed when these bones were inscribed, so the writing system must be much older. Earlier Chinese people would have written on scrolls made from strips of bamboo, which have not survived.

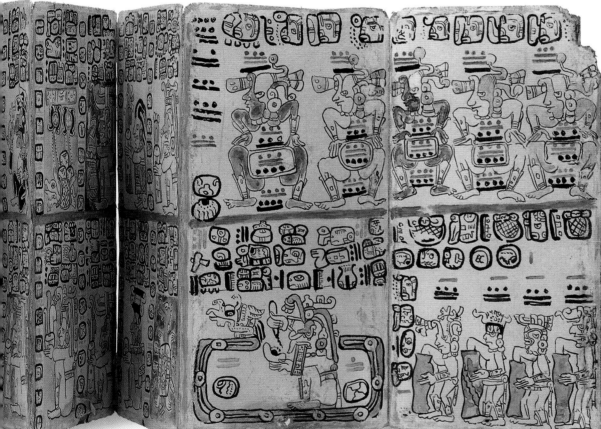

history

▲ MAYAN BOOK
The Maya invented a system with some picture signs standing for words and ideas, and other signs standing for sounds. For example, "balam" (jaguar) could be written with a picture of a jaguar's head, or the signs for the sounds "ba," "la," and "m (a)," or a combination of both picture and sound signs. This is one of just four Mayan books that have survived. It was painted on fig-bark paper, with pages that fold up.

THE FIRST HISTORIAN

Our word "history" comes from the Greek word *historia*, or "inquiry," which was also the title of a book by the Greek writer Herodotus, who lived in the 5th century BCE. Herodotus recorded the history of the Greeks and the customs of neighboring peoples, such as the Scythian nomads. His *Historia* is not only the first real history book, but is also a useful source of information on prehistoric people.

TIMELINE

This timeline shows the most important events in prehistory, including the evolution of early humans, their settlement of Earth, and the invention of new technologies. The letters BCE stand for "Before the Common Era," which began with the birth of Jesus Christ. Years after Christ's birth are given as CE, meaning "Common Era." Almost all dates given are approximate.

6,000,000 BCE
The first bipedal (two-footed) apes evolve in the forests of Africa.

4,000,000 BCE
Australopithecine hominins appear in the dry grasslands of South and East Africa.

2,500,000 BCE
The first toolmaking hominin, *Homo habilis*, evolves from australopithecines.

1,900,000 BCE
Homo ergaster ("working man"), the first hominin with the body size and the proportions of a modern human, appears in Africa.

1,800,000 BCE
Homo erectus ("upright man"), a later form of *Homo ergaster*, moves out of Africa and into Asia.

1,500,000 BCE
The leaf-shaped hand-ax is invented, by *Homo ergaster* or *Homo erectus*, in Africa.

500,000 BCE
Layers of ash and charred animal bones found in caves at *Homo erectus* sites in China and Israel date earliest use of fire to this period.

500,000 BCE
Europe is settled by *Homo heidelbergensis* (named after a skeleton site in Germany), a new species of humans who are also skilled hunters.

200,000–100,000 BCE
Modern humans evolve in Africa.

70,000 BCE
Beginning of the Ice Age; Europe now becomes home to the Neanderthal species of human.

50,000 BCE
Australia settled by modern humans from southeast Asia, making the earliest known boat journeys.

40,000 BCE
Modern humans, called Cro-Magnons, move into Europe, where they live alongside the Neanderthals.

30,000 BCE
Cro-Magnons make the first works of art—cave paintings and carvings of people and animals.

30,000 BCE
Global climate enters a severe cold, dry phase, causing deserts in Africa and Australia to spread. This harsh climate leads to the widespread extinction of many large animal species.

30,000–14,000 BCE
North America is settled by people from Asia. They cross over a land bridge between the two continents, which emerged due to low sea levels.

24,000 BCE
Neanderthals become extinct, victims of the changing climate.

16,000 BCE
Homo floresiensis, a tiny hominin, just 3 ft 4 in (1 m) tall, lives on the island of Flores in Indonesia.

13,000 BCE
The Jomon people of Japan make the oldest known pots.

12,000 BCE
Earliest known grinding stones used in Egypt to make flour from wild grasses.

11,500 BCE
The earliest North American culture appears. The Clovis people—named after Clovis, New Mexico—are big-game hunters, who kill mammoths and other large mammals using beautifully made stone-tipped spears.

10,000–8,000 BCE
The global climate warms and the ice sheets retreat. Forests spread and there is a big increase in open water. The rising sea cuts Britain off from Europe and Japan from Asia. This marks the end of the "Paleolithic" (Old Stone) Age and the beginning of the "Mesolithic" (Middle Stone) Age.

9500 BCE
People in Egypt and the Middle East become settled farmers. This marks the beginning of the "Neolithic" (New Stone) Age. The Mesolithic Age continues in those regions where people remain hunter-gatherers.

8000 BCE
Animals and plants domesticated in South America and Mesoamerica.

7300 BCE
Catal Hoyuk, the earliest known town, with a population of several thousand, is established in Anatolia (now Turkey).

7000 BCE
Farming people in the Middle East produce the first textiles. These are linen, which is made from flax.

6000 BCE
Farming people build the first villages in China.

5000 BCE
People in Europe and western Asia begin to smelt copper, the first metal to be used for making tools.

4500 BCE
Farming spreads to Europe, where people begin to set up large stone monuments called megaliths.

4300 BCE
People begin to mine for flint in Europe.

4000 BCE
Polished stone axes become fashionable and are widely traded in Europe.

4000–3000 BCE
The horse is domesticated on the steppes (grassy plains) of Europe and Asia. This gives people their first fast mode of transportation and opens up the steppes.

3800 BCE
Neolithic farmers build causewayed enclosures across northern Europe.

3600 BCE
West Kennet Long Barrow, a Neolithic gallery grave, is built in England. Its entrance faces the midsummer sunrise.

3500–3000 BCE
Bronze invented in China and western Asia.

3300 BCE
Egyptians invent the first writing system, called hieroglyphs.

3300–3000 BCE
Rows of standing stones set up at Carnac in Brittany, France.

3200 BCE
Newgrange Passage Grave, a huge tomb covered with an earth mound, is built in Ireland. Its entrance faces the midwinter sunrise.

3100 BCE
The Sumerians of Mesopotamia (now southern Iraq) invent a writing system known as cuneiform.

3000 BCE
The people of Egypt are united in a single state ruled by a king called the pharaoh.

3000–2000 BCE
The first large towns are built in China, along the Yellow River. These belong to the Longshan culture, named after the first town to be excavated.

2950 BCE
The first monument is built at Stonehenge in England. It is made up of a circular ditch and bank.

2630–2611 BCE
Pharaoh Djoser builds the first Egyptian pyramid, the world's oldest large-stone building.

2600 BCE
First stones are set up at Stonehenge in England.

2500 BCE
The Harappans, or Indus people, create the world's first planned cities in the Indus valley of northwest India and Pakistan.

2500 BCE
The Chinese begin to write texts on "oracle bones." These bones are later used by Shang kings to ask their ancestors questions about the future.

2500 BCE
Trilithons (structures with two upright stones supporting a horizontal one) are set up at Stonehenge.

2000 BCE
Hunter-gatherers belonging to the Arctic Small Tool Tradition settle the coasts and islands of the Canadian Arctic.

2000 BCE
The Xia dynasty establishes the first kingdom in northern China.

1800 BCE
All Indus cities are abandoned, for reasons that are still unknown.

1600 BCE
Shang dynasty replaces the Xia in China.

1550–1500 BCE
Ironworking begins in the Middle East.

1200 BCE
The Olmecs of Mesoamerica and the people of Chavin de Huantar in Peru create the earliest American civilizations.

1000 BCE
Samoa and Tonga in the Pacific are settled by people from southeast Asia.

800 BCE
The Dorset culture develops in the Arctic. Its people make beautiful animal carvings.

700 BCE
Ironworking spreads to western Europe.

500 BCE
Paracas people on the southern coast of Peru preserve their dead as mummies.

500 BCE
Iron Age people in Europe build new fortifications, such as hillforts.

500 BCE
Zapotecs establish the town of Monte Alban, in southern Mexico.

450 BCE
Steppe nomads bury their dead in kurgans (burial mounds) at Pazyryk in the Altai mountains.

400–420 BCE
The Greek writer Herodotus writes the first history book.

200 BCE
People from either Samoa or Tonga settle the Marquesas islands.

200 BCE
Nazca people of southern Peru make large pictures in the Peruvian desert.

150 BCE
The great city of Teotihuacán is founded in Mexico.

100 CE
The warlike Moche people appear in Peru.

200 CE
The Maya begin to build cities in the jungles of Mesoamerica.

400–700 CE
Marquesans settle Easter Island, Hawaii, Tahiti, and the Cook islands.

683 CE
After ruling for 68 years, the Mayan ruler, King Pacal of Palenque, is buried inside his pyramid.

700 CE
Mound-builders build towns in the Mississippi valley of North America.

750 CE
The Mexican city of Teotihuacán is sacked, burned, and abandoned.

900 CE
The Anasazi people build large compact villages in what is now New Mexico.

900 CE
Most of the Mayan cities are abandoned, for reasons that are unknown.

1000 CE
People living on Easter Island begin to construct large stone statues.

1000 CE
The Thule people spread from Alaska across the Canadian Arctic. They use dog sleds and hunt whales and walruses from skin boats.

1000 CE
The Chimu people of northern Peru conquer the first South American empire.

1050 CE
Polynesians from Tahiti or the Cook Islands discover and settle New Zealand.

1276–1299 CE
Prolonged drought in the Anasazi region of North America leads to the abandonment of villages.

1300 CE
The New Zealand Maori people hunt many large flightless bird species to extinction.

1430–1527 CE
The Incas conquer an empire in Peru.

1600 CE
People in Easter Island cut down their last trees, and can no longer set up statues or build boats.

GLOSSARY

Anthropology The study of humankind, including the structure of human societies, how people live together, and their beliefs.

Archaeology From the Greek for "the study of what is ancient," the scientific study of material remains to learn about the past.

Bronze Age A period of prehistory between the Copper Age and the Iron Age, when bronze was used to make tools. Bronze was invented at different times in different places, beginning in Anatolia (Turkey) around 3500 BCE.

Burial mound An artificial hill of earth or stones built over the remains of the dead.

Causewayed enclosure A large site enclosed by one or more rings of circular ditches. The ditches contain raised paths called causeways.

Chalcolithic Copper-Stone Age, a prehistoric period when the first metal tools, made of copper, were used alongside stone ones. Also called the Copper Age, it began in the Middle East around 5000 BCE.

Copper Age see Chalcolithic.

Cro-Magnon The first modern humans to settle in Europe, around 40,000 years ago. They are named after a cave in France where their bones were found.

Cursus Long ceremonial walkway, bounded by a bank and outer ditch.

DNA Deoxyribonucleic acid, or DNA, found in every living cell. Nuclear DNA, which is passed on from both parents, is found in the nucleus of the cell. Mitochondrial DNA (mtDNA), passed on only from the mother, is found in structures outside the nucleus called mitochondria.

Domestication Process in which plants and animals are brought under human control. Desirable features, such as a sheep's woolly coat, are encouraged by selective breeding.

East Asia The countries and regions of eastern and southeast Asia, especially China, Japan, North Korea, South Korea, and Mongolia.

Evolution Process of gradual development as a species changes to become a different species.

Flint A hard quartz rock, found especially in chalk or limestone, that can be chipped or flaked to make tools.

Gallery grave Neolithic stone tomb with burial chambers, or galleries, off a main passage.

Harpoon Spear used to hunt fish, seals, and whales. It has barbs to prevent it from being dislodged, and a line to retrieve the prey.

Henge Large ceremonial circular enclosure bounded by a bank with an inner ditch.

Hominin The collective term for humans and closely related species, such as *Australopithecus*, *Homo habilis*, and *Homo erectus*.

Indus The river that (today) flows through northern India and Pakistan. Around 2500 BCE, a civilization, including the two cities of Harappa and Mohenjo-Daro, developed on the river plain. This was known as the Indus Valley Civilization or Harappan culture.

Iron Age The period when iron was used to make tools, weapons, and also luxury goods. It began in different times in different parts of the world.

Maya The name of the people and civilization that dominated Central America between 250 and 900 CE.

Megalith Any huge stone monument, including dolmens (which have large flat stones resting on upright ones) and standing stones. The word megalith means "big stone" in Greek.

Mesoamerica "Middle America," a region stretching from central Mexico in the north, down to Guatemala in the south.

Mesolithic "Middle Stone" Age, which began with the end of the last Ice Age 11,000 years ago, and ended with the coming of farming, which happened at different times in different places.

Mesopotamia The area—today in Iraq—between the Tigris and the Euphrates rivers where the world's first cities developed around 3000 BCE.

Microlith A tiny flint blade tool, often set into a bone or wooden handle.

Middle East The term commonly used by archaeologists, geographers, and historians to refer to the southwest Asia region encompassing Turkey, Lebanon, Israel, Iraq, Jordan, Saudi Arabia, and the other countries of the Arabian Peninsula.

Mound An artificial hill made of earth or stones.

Mummy A dead body that has been preserved from decay, either intentionally or by accident.

Native Americans The original peoples of the Americas (before the first European settlers arrived) and their descendants.

Natural selection Natural process in which living things that are best adapted to their environment tend to survive, passing on their features to offspring, while those less well-adapted die out. Natural selection makes living things evolve into new species.

Neanderthal An extinct species of early human closely related to our own species.

Neolithic "New Stone" Age, when farming was invented, which followed the Mesolithic Age. It began in the Near East, around 9500 BCE, and ended with the coming of metal tools, at different times in different places.

Nomads People who spend their lives moving from place to place, seeking pasture for herds of grazing animals. The name comes from a Greek word, *nemo*, meaning "to pasture."

Paleoanthropology The study of ancient humans. Paleoanthropologists study the fossil remains of prehistoric humans and related species.

Paleolithic "Old Stone" Age, which is the earliest period of human prehistory. It began 2.5 million years ago, when the first stone tools were made, and ended around 11,000 years ago.

Passage grave A Neolithic tomb with a long, stone-lined passage leading to a burial chamber.

Pueblo From the Spanish word for "village," the term used to describe the Native American villages of the southwestern United States.

Pyramid A large monument with a square or rectangular base and four triangular sides. Pyramids served as royal tombs in ancient Egypt, and as both temples and tombs in Mesoamerica.

Radiocarbon dating Technique used to discover the age of an organic object, such as a dead body, by measuring the amount of radiocarbon (carbon-14) in it.

Roundhouse A circular house with a conical thatched roof built in Western Europe before the Roman occupation.

Scavenger A creature that eats dead animals that have been killed by another animal.

Selective breeding Improving plants or animals by choosing only those with desirable characteristics to breed.

Solstice The time, at midwinter or midsummer, when the sun is farthest north or south and appears to pause before changing direction.

Standing stone A large stone set upright in the earth, as a marker of some kind. Prehistoric people set up single standing stones, and also arranged them in groups.

Steppe Flat, grassy, treeless plain.

Stone Age The first period of prehistoric human culture, when humans used stone tools. It is divided into the Paleolithic (old), Mesolithic (middle), and Neolithic (new) Stone-Age periods.

Stratigraphy The study of the layers (strata) of soils and human deposits at an archaeological site. The term is also used in geology for the study of rock layers.

Sumerians The people of southern Mesopotamia whose civilization flourished between 3000–2000 BCE. They built the first cities and invented cuneiform writing.

Tundra Treeless region of land lying south of the Arctic ice. Tundra has permanently frozen subsoil, and supports low-growing vegetation, such as lichens and mosses.

Ziggurat A stepped mudbrick temple found in Mesopotamia.

HOMININ WHO'S WHO

Humans are descended from bipedal (two-footed) apes that evolved in Africa six million years ago. The collective term for all human-related species is "hominins." The list below gives details of the most important species.

Sahelanthropus tchadensis
Lived: More than 6 million years ago
Brain capacity: 20 cubic in (350 cubic cm)

In 2001, a well-preserved chimplike skull was found near Lake Chad in Africa. Named *Sahelanthropus tchadensis* (human fossil from the Sahel), this may be the earliest hominin. We do not know if it was bipedal.

Orrorin tugenensis
Lived: 6 million years ago
Brain capacity: unknown

In 2000, fossils of an early bipedal ape, about the size of a chimpanzee, were found in the Tugen hills in Kenya. The shape of its femur (upper leg bone) suggested that it walked upright, while its thick humerus (upper arm bone) suggested that it was also still climbing trees. The first hominins would have spent as much time in the trees as on the ground. It was named *Orrorin*, meaning "original man" in the local language, and *tugenensis*, after the Tugen hills.

Australopithecus afarensis
Lived: 4–3 million years ago
Brain capacity: 27 cubic in (450 cubic cm)

Australopithecines were a family of bipedal apes living in South and East Africa. We know a lot about *Australopithecus afarensis* thanks to the discovery of a female skeleton, nicknamed "Lucy." Although their skulls were apelike, they had small canine teeth like modern humans. *Australopithecus afarensis* was delicately built, and males may have reached a height of 4 ft 9 in (1.5 m), while the females were just 3 ft 3 in (1 m) tall.

Australopithecus africanus
Lived: 3–2 million years ago
Brain capacity: 30½ cubic in (500 cubic cm)

Australopithecus africanus ("southern ape from Africa") was the first australopithecine species discovered by Raymond Dart in 1924. A delicately built species, the males were around 4 ft 6 in (1.4 m) tall, while females were perhaps 3 ft 9 in (1.2 m) tall.

Australopithecus boisei
Lived: 2.3–1.4 million years ago
Brain capacity: 33½ cubic in (550 cubic cm)

Australopithecus boisei (named after anthropologist Charles Boise), which lived in East Africa, belonged to a more heavily built species than the earlier australopithecines. Some experts believe they were so different that they should be classed separately, as *Paranthropus* ("alongside the human") *boisei*. Nicknamed "Nutcracker Man" after its massive chewing teeth, it had a ridge across its skull, called a sagittal crest, for the attachment of chewing muscles. It was the same height as *Australopithecus africanus*.

Australopithecus robustus
Lived: 1.8–1 million years ago
Brain capacity: 33½ cubic in (550 cubic cm)

As the name "robust," or strongly built, suggests, *Australopithecus robustus* was another heavily built species. It lived in South Africa and, like *Australopithecus boisei*, had a sagittal crest. Some experts call this species *Paranthropus robustus*. The males were around 4 ft 3 in (1.3 m) tall, while females were 3 ft 3 in (1 m) tall.

Homo habilis
Lived: 2.5–1.6 million years ago
Brain capacity: 42 cubic in (687 cubic cm)

Homo habilis ("handy man") had a more human-shaped skull, with a larger brain and smaller teeth than the australopithecines. These were the first hominins to make stone tools. Despite their human features, they had short legs and long arms. The males, at 4 ft (1.2 m), were bigger than females, who were only 3 ft 3 in (1 m) tall.

Homo rudolfensis
Lived: 2.3–1.8 million years ago
Brain capacity: 46 cubic in (750 cubic cm)

Homo rudolfensis was named after Lake Rudolf (now Lake Turkana) in Kenya, where its skull was found. This was a hominin with a larger brain, flatter face, and bigger front teeth than *Homo habilis*. Yet the two species are so similar that they are grouped together, as "habilines." Both species lived in East Africa and both made tools. Habilines would have eaten much more meat than australopithecines.

Homo ergaster
Lived: 1.9 million to perhaps 600,000 years ago
Brain capacity: 55 cubic in (900 cubic cm)

Homo ergaster ("working man") was the first hominin to have the modern human body size and proportions, with long legs and short arms. Yet their skulls had projecting jaws and low flat foreheads, like an ape. Excellent toolmakers, they probably invented the leaf-shaped hand-ax.

Homo erectus
Lived: 1.8 million to perhaps 50,000 years ago
Brain capacity: 76 cubic in (1,250 cubic cm)

Homo ergaster evolved to become the larger-brained *Homo erectus* ("upright man"), which had a low flat skull with shelflike brow ridges. These were the first humans to leave Africa and move into Asia. They also learned how to control fire. *Homo erectus* evolved with regional differences. Chinese *Homo erectus*, known as "Peking Man," had a flatter face and more rounded skull than the southeast Asian variety, called "Java Man."

Homo heidelbergensis
Lived: 600,000–400,000 years ago
Brain capacity: 79 cubic in (1,300 cubic cm)

Homo heidelbergensis, named after Heidelberg in Germany, where its remains were first found, was the first human species to move into Europe. Like *Homo erectus*, *Homo heidelbergensis* had pronounced brow ridges, but these were curving rather than the flatter shelflike ridges of the earlier species. One of their best-known sites is Boxgrove in England where, 500,000 years ago, *Homo heidelbergensis* hunted elephants and rhinos. Finds of two teeth and a shin bone from Boxgrove are the oldest human remains found in Britain.

Homo rhodesiensis
Lived: 600,000–125,000 years ago
Brain capacity: 95 cubic in (1,550 cubic cm)

Homo rhodesiensis ("Rhodesian man") is the name given to a skull found in 1924, in a mine in what was then Rhodesia but is now Zimbabwe. The skull has the largest brow ridges of any hominin, yet its brain was the size of a modern human's. Some experts believe that it belongs to the *Homo heidelbergensis* species.

Homo neanderthalensis
Lived 100,000–24,000 years ago
Brain capacity: 95 cubic in (1,550 cubic cm)

The Neanderthal, which lived across Europe and western Asia, was a human that had adapted to the cold of the last Ice Age. Neanderthals were short, stocky, and very strong. They had projecting midfaces, with large noses and receding chins. Their brains were the same size as those of modern humans. They cared for their old and sick, wore animal skin clothes, and buried their dead in caves.

Homo floresiensis
Lived: 16,000 years ago
Brain capacity: 23 cubic in (380 cubic cm)

Homo floresiensis ("man from Flores") is the name given to a previously unknown hominin, whose skull was found on the Indonesian island of Flores in 2003. The individual, nicknamed the "Hobbit," was just 3 ft 4 in (1 m) tall, and hunted giant rats, that are still found on the island. Despite its unusually small brain, its skull shape and use of tools show that it was another human.

Homo sapiens
Lived: 200,000 BCE to the present
Brain capacity: 55–122 cubic in (900–2,000 cubic cm)—average 82 cubic in (1,350 cubic cm)

Homo sapiens ("wise man") is the name of our own species. We are distinct from earlier hominins in having a high forehead, with slight brow ridges, a projecting chin, and a small face mounted beneath the front of the braincase. We are the only hominin species left on the planet, and there are now 6.6 billion of us.

INDEX

A page number in **bold** refers to the main entry of that subject.

ACKNOWLEDGMENTS

Dorling Kindersley would like to thank Christine Heilman for Americanization.

Dorling Kindersley Ltd. is not responsible and does not accept liability for the availability or content of any website other than its own, or for any exposure to offensive, harmful or inaccurate material that may appear on the Internet. Dorling Kindersley Ltd. will have no liability for any damage or loss caused by viruses that may be downloaded as a result of looking at and browsing the websites that it recommends. Dorling Kindersley downloadable images are the sole copyright of Dorling Kindersley Ltd. and may not be reproduced, stored, or transmitted in any form or by any means for any commercial or profit-related purpose without prior written permission of the copyright owner.

Picture Credits

The publisher would like to thank the following for their kind permission to reproduce their photographs:

Abbreviations key:
a-above, b-below/bottom, c-center, f-far, l-left, r-right, t-top

1–2 DK Images: The Natural History Museum, London. **2** DK Images: Rowan Greenwood. **3** Ancient Art & Architecture Collection: Ronald Sheridan. **4–5** DK Images: Sean Hunter. **7** DK Images: National Museum, New Delhi (br). **8** Corbis: William Campbell/Sygma (cl). DK Images: National Museum of Copenhagen (l). **8–9** DK Images: Rowan Greenwood (bc). **9** Corbis: Peter Jackson (t). PA Photos: AP (cr). **10** Alamy Images: Homer Sykes (cr). DK Images: Barrie Watts (bc). Museum of London Archaeology Service: Andy Chopping (bl). **11** Corbis: Skyscan (bl). DK Images: The British Museum/Peter Hayman (tl). **12** Scottish National Portrait Gallery: Sir Henry Raeburn: Portrait of James Hutton, 1727-1797 (detail, bl). **13** Alamy Images: Superlic (bl). The Bridgeman Art Library: Engraved by Albert Newsam (after)/The Royal Institution, UK (br). Tate, London: Francis Danby 1793-1861: The Deluge (tr). **14** Corbis: Bettmann (tr, cr). The Natural History Museum, London: (bl). **15** The Bridgeman Art Library: Geological Society, London (b). The Natural History Museum, London: (c). **16** Corbis: Wolfgang Kaehler (r). The Natural History Museum, London: (bl). **17** Getty Images: National Geographic (bl). The Natural History Museum, London: (r). **18–19** The Natural History Museum, London: (b). **19** The Natural History Museum, London: (tl). Photoshot/NHPA: Steve Robinson (tr). **21** The Natural History Museum, London: (br). **22** Corbis: Bettmann (bl). PA Photos: Frank Franklin/AP (br). **23** DK Images: The Natural History Museum (tl). **24** The Art Archive: Musée des Antiquités, St.Germain en Laye/Dagli Orti (clb). The Bridgeman Art Library: Musée des Antiquités, St.Germain en Laye (br). DK Images: The Natural History Museum, London (cr). The Natural History Museum, London: (cla). **25** The Natural History Museum, London: (b). **26** Corbis: Roger Ressmeyer (crb). The Natural History Museum, London: (cl, bc). Science Photo Library: Alain Pol, ISM (cra). **26–27** The Natural History Museum, London: (t). **27** Alamy Images: Nick Greaves (b). Corbis: Jan Woitas (cr). **28** akg-images: (c). Corbis: Staffan Widstrand (tl). **29** The Natural History Museum, London: (tr). RIA Novosti: (tl). **30–31** PA Photos: AP (b). **31** Ancient Art & Architecture Collection: Ronald Sheridan (tl). Ulmer Museum: (r). **33** PA Photos: AP/University of Melbourne (tl). Robert Harding Picture Library: James Hager (tr). **35** Corbis: Paul A.Souders (r). PA Photos: AP/Elaine Thompson (cl); Perfect Image/James Chatters (bc). **36** Alamy Images: Ariadne Van Zandbergen/Robert Estall (cr). DK Images: The British Museum (cl). **36–37** Image courtesy of thedesigndesk.co.uk: (b). **37** DK Images: Dan Bannister Collection (tr). Heritage Images: The British Museum (br). **38** Alamy Images: Jack Sullivan (tr). **39** The Bridgeman Art Library: Ashmolean Museum, University of Oxford, UK (bl). **40** Alamy Images: Giles Moberly (bc). **41** The Bridgeman Art Library: Museum of Fine Arts, Boston, Massachusetts, USA/E. Rhodes and Leona B. Carpenter Foundation Grant (r). Heritage Images: The Print Collector (bl). **42–43** Alamy Images: Images & Stories (c). Catalhoyuk Research Project / John Swogger: (t). **43** Alamy Images: Images & Stories (cr). **44** The Bridgeman Art Library: Louvre, Paris, France (bl). Corbis: Ed Kashi (br). **46** Alamy Images: Chris Crumley (t). DK Images: The British Museum (cr, br). **47** DK Images: The British Museum (b). Werner Forman Archive: Egyptian Museum, Cairo (l). **48** akg-images: Gerard Degeorge (b). **49** akg-images: Jean-Louis Nou (l). **50** Claire Boulter: (cr). Corbis: Julia Waterlow/Eye Ebiquitous (t). **51** The Bridgeman Art Library: People's Republic of China/Lauros Giraudon (r). Corbis: Chinese Academy of Science/Reuters (cr); Dean Conger (bl). **53** Institute of Archaeology and Cultural Relics: (r). **54** Alamy Images: Robert Estall (tr). **55** Alamy Images: Leslie Garland Picture Library (cl); Homer Sykes (bl). **56** The English Heritage Photo Library: (tl); NMR (cr). Last Refuge: Dae Sasitorn (cl). **57** The English Heritage Photo Library: (cl, c, cr). **58** Alamy Images: Skyscan Photolibrary (tr). Ancient Art & Architecture Collection: Ronald Sheridan (b). The English Heritage Photo Library: Judith Dobie (c). **59** Robert Harding Picture Library: Roy Rainford (t). **60–61** Ancient Art & Architecture Collection: M.Andrews (t). The Bridgeman Art Library: Ashmolean Museum, University of Oxford, UK (b). **61** South Tyrol Museum Of Archaeology: (tl, br, cr, fbr). **63** Corbis: Homer Sykes (t). Dover Museum: (bl). Wiltshire Heritage Museum: (c, cl, cr). **64** akg-images: Erich Lessing (bc). **65** akg-images: John Hios (tr). The Bridgeman Art Library: Ashmolean Museum, University of Oxford, UK (bl). **66** The Art Archive: Archaeological Museum, Chora, Greece/Dagli Orti/ Piet de Jong (tl). **67** akg-images: National Archaeological Museum, Athens, Greece (detail, b). Ancient Art & Architecture Collection: Ronald Sheridan (tl). The Bridgeman Art Library: National Archaeological Museum, Athens, Greece (tr). **68** The Bridgeman Art Library: Egyptian National Museum, Cairo (tl). **69** akg-images: Erich Lessing (bl). Alamy Images: Blom Aerofilms Ltd (tr); David Chapman (br). **70** Alamy Images: J.Marshall/Tribaleye Images (fcr). **71** Alamy Images: PhotoStockFile (bl). OSF: (tl). **72** Werner Forman Archive: Museum of the American Indian, Heye Foundation, New York (cr); Smithsonian Institution, Washington (bl). **73** Nick Carlson/Julio L. Betancourt/US Geological Survey: (br). **74** akg-images: Veintimilla (bl). **75** Corbis: Nik Wheeler (bl). Getty Images: National Geographic (cl). **76** Alamy Images: Archivberlin Fotoagentur (bl). **76–77** Getty Images: Kenneth Garrett/National Geographic (c). **77** The Bridgeman Art Library: Alan Gillam/Mexicolore (br). Werner Forman Archive: The British Museum (cl); National Museum of Archaeology, Mexico City (tr). **78** Alamy Images: Visual Arts Library, London (cr). Corbis: Charles & Josette Lenars (bl). **79** Corbis: Werner Forman (bl); Kevin Schafer (r); Karen Su (tl). **80** Alamy Images: Gary Cook (tl). Corbis: Gianni Dagli Orti (bl). **81** Alamy Images: Glen Alison (tl); Pep Roig (tr). **82** Corbis: Michel Setboun (t). **83** The Bridgeman Art Library: Hermitage, St. Petersburg, Russia (tr); Private Collection (br). Corbis: Charles O'Rear (bl). DK Images: Judith Miller/Sloan's (crb). Getty Images: National Geographic (cr). Panos Pictures: Georg Gerster (tl). **84** Bryan and Cherry Alexander Photography: (cl). **85** Bryan and Cherry Alexander Photography: (tr). Heritage Images: The British Museum (br). **86** Ardea: Alan Greensmith (fbr). Corbis: Wolfgang Kaehler (bl, br). Heritage Images: The British Museum (cr). Robert Harding Picture Library: Sylvain Grandadam (fbl). **87** Werner Forman Archive: The British Museum (tl). **88** DK Images: The British Museum (tl); Judith Miller/Ancient Art (cla). **89** DK Images: The British Museum (tl)

Jacket images
Front: Getty Images: Taxi/Vladimir Pcholkin. **Back**: Getty Images: The Bridgeman Art Library/Prehistoric (cr); Science Photo Library: Mauricio Anton (fcr); Christian Darkin (fcl); John Reader (cl). **Spine**: Getty Images: Taxi/Vladimir Pcholkin.

All other images © Dorling Kindersley For further information, see: **www.dkimages.com**